This is a great book. In one sense *Who Needs the Church?* is 'just' a simple look at what the Bible says about the church. But it adds up to a compelling and exciting vision for the local church, for your local congregation. If you're feeling sceptical and jaded about the church, then this book will renew your enthusiasm. It will help you to see afresh that the 'ordinary' life of an 'ordinary' church is actually something extraordinary, filled with Christ's supernatural presence and power.

Tim Chester
Senior Faculty, Crosslands Training

The global pandemic has been spiritually very revealing – not least in showing how many Christians have a low view of the church. This book is a timely call to a biblical understanding of what it means to belong to the body and bride of Christ, and the blessings that come from gathering physically as God's people.

Robin Weekes
Minister, Emmanuel Church Wimbledon, London

Terry Johnson's book, *Who Needs the Church?* could not have been written at a more urgent moment. The endemic cultural individualism of the twenty-first century, coupled with a sudden provision of online services has provoked a reassessment of the nature and importance of church, and has led to new, unhealthy Sunday habits. In short, accessible chapters, Johnson carefully restores church to its rightful and central place.

Iver Martin
Principal, Edinburgh Theological Seminary
Edinburgh, Scotland

Confusion is swarming around the meaning and necessity of the local church. Now more than ever, evangelicals desperately need better and clearer ecclesiology. Pastor Terry Johnson has done that in this book!

Written with provocative apologetic flair, Pastor Terry Johnson informs his readers that the church is not a voluntary institution, but a living organism to which we must belong. He clearly argues from scripture that, 'To be a Christian is to be a member of the church. To be outside of the church, therefore, is still to be in the realm of darkness.'

You will walk away from this resource not only better informed biblically, but encouraged and motivated to invest deeply in the bride of Christ, the church of God.

Erin Wheeler
Author of *The Good Portion –*
The Church: Delighting in the Doctrine of the Church

At times a book is desirable because of the author and at other times because of the subject. I commend this volume to you because of both the author and the subject. When God saves us He saves us personally and He saves us to engage us and place us in a local church which is a testimony of the body of Christ. The biblical rationale and necessity, as well as the blessings of being a vital participant in the body of Christ, are affirmed though biblical faithfulness and clarity by the author, Terry Johnson. This book will not only enhance your growth in grace but will become an instrument as you disciple others in Christ's Church.

Harry L. Reeder, III
Pastor Teacher, Briarwood Presbyterian Church, Birmingham, Alabama

Why we need the Church
(and why the Church needs us)

WHO NEEDS THE
CHURCH?

TERRY JOHNSON

CHRISTIAN
FOCUS

Copyright © Terry L. Johnson 2022

hardback ISBN 978-1-5271-0835-6
ebook ISBN 978-1-5271-0903-2

Published in 2022
by
Christian Focus Publications Ltd,
Geanies House, Fearn, Ross-shire,
IV20 1TW, Scotland, U.K.
www.christianfocus.com

Cover design by Pete Barnsley

Printed and bound by Gutenberg, Malta

Contents

I
Introduction

1

Our Collapsing Ecclesiology

It's Sunday morning. You wake up, prepare a hot beverage, eat breakfast, and finish your morning routine. Now what? Go to church? Maybe, maybe not. May depend on what else is going on. Or what I feel like. Or what is available online. Attending public worship services has become optional for a growing number of professing Christians, as has commitment to the visible, institutional church.

Churchless Christianity

It has been reported for years that a number of high-profile evangelicals only rarely attend church. They may have 'accountability' groups, or prayer groups, or small-group Bible studies, in which they participate. They may watch church on the television or listen to sermons online. However, the local, visible church is optional for them and many, many others. 'A gated community in the evangelical world,' USA Today announced. 'Many of the nation's most powerful believers … won't be found in the pews … creating a growing gap between them and 'the people.'[1] Julia Duin documented a wider problem involving low profile evangelicals as well, prompting her book-length response, *Quitting Church*.[2] The pandemic of 2020-2021 has taken this ominous trend and put it on steroids. Many of the faithful have enjoyed stumbling downstairs five minutes before worship, still in their pajamas, easing into a comfortable chair, latte in hand, and watching a YouTube church service, their own church or some other, without ever having to leave their house.

Popular pollster, George Barna, greeted the new millennia by all but proposing the abolition of the local church in his book *Revolution*, as he attempted to convince the Church (large 'C') to ride yet another cultural trend to success.[3] Having already provided significant demographic fuel for the megachurch phenomena of the 1980s and 90s,[4] he introduced yet another re-creation of the church for the 2000s, presumably to correct the failures of the market-driven approach he had previously championed. The problem with the church (presumably the purpose-driven,

1. D. Michael Lindsay, 'A gated community in the evangelical world,' *USA Today*, (February 18, 2008), 13A.

2. Julia Duin, *Quitting Church: Why the Faithful are Fleeing and What to do About It* (Grand Rapids, Michigan: Baker Books, 2008).

3. George Barna, *Revolution* (Carol Stream, IL: Tyndale House Publishers, 2005).

4. As in his books *Marketing the Church: What They Never Taught You about Church Growth* (Colorado Springs: Nav Press, 1988); *User Friendly Churches: What Christians Need to Know About the Churches People Love to Go To* (Ventura: Regal Books, 1992).

market-driven church he helped create), he said, is that while it 'can be instrumental in bringing us closer to (God) … the research data clearly shows churches are not doing the job. If the local church is the hope of the world, then the world has no hope.'[5] He spoke breathlessly of 'the Revolution,' of 'an unprecedented reengineering of America's faith,' of 'the most significant recalibration of the American Christian body in more than a century,' of a movement 'to advance the church and to redefine the church.'[6] He announced the emergence of the 'New Church,'[7] which, in fact, is no church at all. Church, as 'traditionally' understood, was for Barna a human institution, not a biblical one. The new church, as he construed it, is without structure, organization, clergy, officers, accountability or discipline. It has no location, commitments, or physical presence. It is merely an informal, *ad hoc*, uncovenanted association of believers. For 'revolutionaries' the local church ceases to exist. The requirements of Hebrews 10:25 (that believers assemble together) could be fulfilled, he says, 'in a worship service or at Starbucks.'[8] His revolutionaries affirm, 'I am not called to attend or join a church. I am called to be the church.'[9] The result, he assures us, will be the robust spiritual life, ministry, and relationships that have eluded us thus far.

---

5. Barna, *Revolution*, 36.

6. Ibid., viii-x.

7. Ibid., 42.

8. Ibid., 114.

9. Ibid., 129.

Common practice

The eccentricities of the highly influential Barna are matched by the commonplace practices of the growing numbers of unaffiliated and non-attending believers. Overall, church attendance rates have been declining since the early 1960s, a trend that has accelerated in the last two decades. Church, for many, is like the local gym, except one actually has to join the local gym and pay fees. It's good to go there to exercise, but sometimes one can do just as well at home. Or maybe somewhere else? Or where one's 'needs' will be met? Attend when it is convenient. Attend elsewhere or nowhere when it is not convenient. These are the commonplace comments that we hear.

No doubt the church, for its part, has, in no small way, contributed to its perceived irrelevance. Its hypocrisy has undermined its moral integrity; its legalism has forfeited its pastoral role; its forays into politics have diluted its mission; and its pandering to the culture has compromised its message. 'Churchianity' is the contemptuous term many serious Christians have used to describe formalistic religion. No wonder scores of sincere believers are looking elsewhere. Still, the question that should be raised is this: can this dismissive outlook be squared with that of the New Testament? Even more specifically, can it be squared with the outlook and intention of Jesus?

II
What Scripture Teaches

2

Jesus and the Church

How many times does Jesus mention the church? I've asked that question in a number of forums (Reformed University Fellowship, Sunday School, Drug Court Bible Study, Sunday morning pulpit, various conferences, etc.), and gotten answers ranging from thirty-six to six. Surprise is the typical response when I reveal that Jesus in the whole of His earthly ministry mentions the church, specifically the *ekklesia*, only twice.[1] Initially this seems to confirm the bias of those who say they admire Jesus but have minimal regard for the church. The church, they say, is man's invention. Jesus said little about the church. He didn't intend to found a church. We've built an ecclesiastical mountain out of an exegetical molehill, they insist. We follow Jesus, they claim, but have discarded the millstone that the church has become around His message.

What should we say about this? Simply that Jesus' words about the church must be weighed, not merely counted. Essentially, Jesus says two things about the

---

1. We are setting aside for now Jesus' extensive teaching on the Kingdom or Reign of God, which bears upon, but is not coextensive with, the church.

church: In Matthew 16:18 He says, 'I will build my church.' In Matthew 18:17 He says, 'Tell it to the church.' Take them in order.

I WILL BUILD MY CHURCH

> And I tell you, you are Peter, and on this rock I will build my church, and the gates of hell shall not prevail against it (Matt. 16:18).

Having heard Peter's great confession of Jesus' identity, what does Christ promise to build? His church. Anything else? No. He promises to build no other earthly institution, no other worldly entity. He is not building a school, a business, a charity, or a legal enterprise. He attaches His personal pronoun 'my' to no other earthly entity. He does not speak of 'my' nation, or family, or business, or political party. He does not attach His name or reputation to a political cause or movement or legislation. Jesus sums up His entire mission as church-building. This is His chief concern. When we arrive at the end of the Bible, we find that the work that Jesus came to do, that of building His church, has been completed:

> And I saw the holy city, new Jerusalem, coming down out of heaven from God, prepared as a bride adorned for her husband (Rev. 21:2).

The church, the 'holy city,' the 'new Jerusalem' (cf. 3:12; Gal. 4:26), the 'bride' of Christ (cf. 21:9; 19:7; Eph. 5:22-32), descends from heaven, pure, perfected, completed, 'in all her glory' (Eph. 5:27, NASB). What is Jesus doing, incarnation and post-incarnation, through His atonement then and His mediation now? Building His church.

What is Jesus using this church to do? It is His tool, His weapon, by which He will batter down the 'gates of hell' and destroy the devil's strongholds (2 Cor. 10:4). Hell's 'gates,' its powers, will not 'prevail' against the church as it pursues its mission. The powers of evil that were dealt a death blow through the cross (Col. 2:15; Eph. 1:21) will see their destruction consummated through the activities of the church. This eradication of evil will be realized both in individual hearts through gospel proclamation and on a worldwide scale through missions (Matt. 28:18-20).

TELL IT TO THE CHURCH
Let's move to the second reference.

> If your brother sins against you, go and tell him his fault, between you and him alone. If he listens to you, you have gained your brother. But if he does not listen, take one or two others along with you, that every charge may be established by the evidence of two or three witnesses. If he refuses to listen to them, tell it to the church. And if he refuses to listen even to the church, let him be to you as a Gentile and a tax collector (Matt. 18:15-17).

What does Jesus want us to tell to the church? He speaks of the problem of a sinning 'brother' who refuses to heed admonition, who refuses to repent. His obstinacy must be revealed to the church which must act to disassociate him: 'Let him be to you as a Gentile or a tax collector' (Matt. 18:17).

What is assumed or implied by this second reference to the *ekklesia*? More than most have imagined. The church that Jesus envisions has: 1) standards of belief and conduct to which participants are expected to conform; 2) membership, with clear guidelines about who is to be included or excluded; 3) a process of discipline which evaluates misbehavior and errant beliefs; 4) a form of government; 5) meetings at which a pertinent matter may be discussed; 6) officers who administer the whole. Jesus speaks in these two passages of committing to the church the keys of the kingdom of heaven (Matt. 16:19) and the power of binding and loosing (Matt. 16:19 and Matt. 18:18; cf. John 20:23). The church that Jesus envisions has concrete existence, bricks and mortar, one might say. It is an organization. It is an institution. It has members. It has leaders. Its members are committed to each other, to their leaders, to the Triune God whose church it is, and to the church itself as something greater than the sum of its parts.

The church that Jesus builds is not merely an informal gathering of believers at a coffee shop to pray and share Scripture verses. Such meetings are self-selecting; the church is not. Participants choose those with whom they will join in such meetings, typically according to common interests. However, the New Testament church looks nothing like an organization built along lines of affinity, except affinity for Christ. The numberless multitude in heaven consists of believers 'from every nation, from all tribes and peoples and languages' (Rev. 7:9). Many of the problems found in the New

Testament, with which the apostles and the epistles were dealing, arose precisely because of the diversity of age, class, and ethnicity of the members of the church (e.g. Acts 6:1-7; 15:1ff; Gal. 1–3; Titus 2; James 4; etc.). Informal gatherings also lack accountability. One may simply stop participating and walk out of the lives of those with whom one has been involved.

Because Jesus' words imply membership, standards, leadership and discipline, they suggest the mutual accountability and mutual responsibility of covenanted relationships. When leading evangelicals say, 'Don't go to church: be the church,' their leading is misleading. The gathering of two or three in Jesus' name is the same entity that excommunicates (Matt. 18:20, 18:17). We repeat: that entity has a government. It has a form of discipline. It has membership. It has standards of belief and conduct. One can be included or excluded from this church with eternal repercussions (certainly implied by the keys mentioned in Matt. 16:19; see also 1 Cor. 5:12; 6:4). It has meetings in which it is constituted as the 'church.' 'When you come together as a church,' the Apostle Paul says. 'As a church' indicates the church assembled formally, officially as a congregation under the direction of the elders (e.g. 1 Cor. 11:18; 5:4; 11:17, 20, 33, 34; 14:26). This is not to be confused with when private Christians 'come together' informally, unofficially, or spontaneously. Informal gatherings of Christians may be helpful. Interdenominational community Bible studies may be edifying. However, they are not the church. The intimate bonds created through group Bible studies and

19

prayer primarily are meant to be forged in the context of the church to which we belong, where we can depend on others and others can depend on us, where I have covenanted to be there for you, and you for me.

Don't merely count Jesus' words regarding the church. Weigh them. Like silver. Like gold. How can I commit to the church, one may object, when the church is so flawed? It is so shallow, so corrupt, so hurtful, so compromised, many insist. Indeed, we concede, at times it is. However, our question is, did Jesus not know this? When He established the church, did He not know that there would be problems? That there would be rivalry and infighting? That there would be hypocrisy and hurt? Of course He did. Nevertheless, He said what He said, calling us into the church and to be devoted to its people and mission.

We suffer today for lack of an ecclesiology. A family leaves a congregation with which it has been associated for over a decade, without warning and without explanation. The members who are left behind are bewildered. They may have sacrificed for that family during a time of crisis. Prayers were offered, visits made, meals cooked, funds given, and baby-sitting provided. Gone. Why? Because they, like so many others, see the church as a voluntary association, like a health club, rather than a commitment, like marriage.

A serious hole exists in our Christian discipleship if we are not fully committed to building the church as Jesus envisioned it, where I am accountable to others and they are accountable to me; where I am responsible to others and they are responsible to me; where I can count on them, and they can count on me.

3
Keys of the Kingdom

Is there more to be learned from Jesus' foundation teaching on the *ekklesia*, the church? Indeed there is, and we can continue our investigations by asking ourselves a very basic question: How is it that we get the benefits of what Jesus accomplished on the cross? By what means do those benefits flow to us today? This is a valuable question to ask and a crucial one to answer. After all, the events of the cross (death, burial, resurrection, ascension) took place long ago and far away. Two thousand years have passed. Most of us must cross oceans and/or land masses to get to the place where the redemptive acts occurred. How do His benefits span all that time and all that space to get to us today?

The biblical answer is that the grace of Christ is communicated to us through the God-ordained 'means of grace.' God has given *means* through which He imparts the *grace* of Christ. He doesn't ordinarily call out to us from heaven or zap us with grace directly, though He did in the case of the Apostle Paul. No, *ordinarily* (a

21

favorite word among Reformed Protestants), He uses means. He uses human agency. He provides spiritual tools for spiritual work.

PRIMARY MEANS

What are those means? We have touched on this already, but now is the time to give this question focused attention. Almost *anything* can be a means of grace. Marriage, for example, may be a means. So also may divorce. I know a man whose divorce led directly to his conversion! Events and relationships along the whole spectrum, from adversity to prosperity, may be means of grace. 'It was good for me that I was afflicted,' the psalmist recognizes (Ps. 119:71). Our concern, however, is with the *primary* means. What are the central, the crucial, the core and ordained means that God uses to save and sanctify His people?

The traditional answer is the word, sacraments, and prayer. There are three and only three *primary* means. We may also refer to these as the *promised* means. God promises to use His *word* (in its various forms: read, sung, prayed, and especially preached), the *sacraments* (understood as visible words), and *prayer*. Through those three primary means, God saves and sanctifies His people.

KEYS OF THE KINGDOM

Where *primarily* are the primary means operative? We may now move on to Jesus' next statement and the next verse in Matthew 16:

> I will give you the keys of the kingdom of heaven,
> and whatever you bind on earth shall be bound in
> heaven, and whatever you loose on earth shall be loosed
> in heaven' (Matt. 16:19).

The sphere in which they primarily function is the church. God imparts His grace through the ministry of the church. The 'you' to whom Jesus gave the 'keys of the kingdom of heaven' is the church (Matt. 16:19). These '*keys*' lock and unlock the gates of heaven.[1] Traditionally, they have been understood as the aforementioned means of grace. The word, verbal (read, preached, sung, prayed) and visible (sacraments), is the key. 'The gate of life is only opened to us by the Word of God,' says Calvin.[2] The Puritan Matthew Poole (1624-1679) identifies the keys with 'the whole administration of the gospel.'[3] Through the gospel word, those dead in trespasses and sin are born again (1 Pet. 1:23-25), spiritual babes are fed (1 Pet. 2:1ff), and saints are sanctified (John 17:17). Faith comes by 'hearing the word of Christ' (Rom 10:17). Christ has placed His word, the key, into the hands of the church.

---

1. For a recent exposition of the meaning of the 'keys,' see Gary Prentiss Waters, *How Jesus Runs the Church* (Phillipsburg, NJ: P & R Publishing, 2011), 13-16.

2. John Calvin, *A Harmony of the Gospels: Matthew, Mark, and Luke,* Vols. I-III (1555; Grand Rapids: William B. Eerdmans Publishing Co., 1972), II:87.

3. Matthew Poole, *Commentary on the Holy Bible* , Vols. I-III (1683-85; London: The Banner of Truth Trust, 1963), III:77.

Consequently, preachers must be 'sent' if unbelievers are to hear. Note, they don't merely *go*. They are *sent*. Who sends them? The church.

> And how are they to hear without someone preaching? And how are they to preach unless they are sent? (Rom. 10:14b-15a).

The church assesses the qualifications of leaders (1 Tim. 3; Titus 1). The church ordains, authorizes, and sends preachers, such as Paul and Barnabas (Acts 13:1-4). The church places the key into the hands of those called by God to preach.

BINDING AND LOOSING

Further, the church is given the power of binding and loosing. Jesus says,

> Whatever you bind on earth shall be bound in heaven, and whatever you loose on earth shall be loosed in heaven (Matt. 16:19b).

Modern commentators argue that 'binding' and 'loosing' are technical terms used by the rabbis to declare what was permitted and not permitted. New Testament scholar, Leon Morris, (1914-2006) explains,

> The saying means that the Spirit-inspired church will be able to declare authoritatively what things are forbidden and what things are permitted. [4]

---

4. Leon Morris, *The Gospel According to Matthew* (Grand Rapids: William B. Eerdmans Publishing Co., 1992), 426.

To proclaim gospel truth is to 'loose,' or to liberate those who believe (John 8:32). The gospel frees sinners from bondage to sin, even as it leaves the unrepentant bound in darkness. This power of the church, whatever the nuance, is a declarative power of eternal consequence. Through proclamation and discipline, the kingdom of God is opened and closed, heaven's gates are unlocked and locked, and sinners, in turn, liberated or bound, included or excluded.

Baptizing and membership

Moreover, the church baptizes new believers into its fellowship. 'What shall we do?' is the cry of those convicted of their sins (Acts 2:37). The answer of Peter is surprising for those thinking along typically modern and narrowly individualistic lines. 'Repent and be baptized,' he urges (Acts 2:38). This is the consistent pattern. Baptism, like circumcision before it, is the rite of admission into the community of the people of God (Col. 2:11; Rom. 4:11). Those who believe are baptized and added to the number of the church (Acts 2:41, 47). The Samaritans (8:17), the Ethiopian eunuch (8:36, 38), Saul of Tarsus (9:18), Cornelius (10:47, 48), Lydia and her household (16:15), and the Philippian jailer and his household (16:33) are all baptized into the membership of the church. It is accurate to say that the Book of Acts does not recognize churchless Christianity. To be a Christian is to be a member of the church. To be outside of the church, therefore, is still to be in the realm of darkness (Col. 1:13). Those removed from the church are said to be 'deliver(ed) to Satan' (1 Cor. 5:5), to the 'god of this world' who blinds the minds of unbelievers (2 Cor. 4:4). Outside of the church, the key is unavailable, heaven remains locked, and salvation unavailable. Outside of the church, 'there is no ordinary possibility of salvation,' the Westminster Confession of Faith maintains (XXV.2).

VITAL

Want to be admitted into heaven? The church has the key that unlocks the door. Jesus is the door (John 10:7), but the church has the key. The health, the well-being, the growth of every believer is dependent upon the ministry of the church. Joining the church should never be considered dismissively. Actively participating in – and contributing to – the life and ministry of the church should never be considered optional. Because Jesus has committed the keys of the kingdom to the church of God, every believer must go to the church to receive that ministry which will feed and sustain his or her soul.

Someone may object: I get more out of my Bible study group than I do the ministry of the church. Another may object: I get more out of my quiet time than I do out of church. Still others may object: I get more out of listening to my favorite preacher online than I do out of church. All three objectors may then proceed wrongly to order their priorities according to their perceptions, abandoning the local church in the process. All three may conclude that the church is expendable in light of the greater utility of their preferred alternative.

Our answer? The alternatives to the church are not the same as the church, whatever our perceptions may be. The sacraments are not available online. Neither are they of secondary importance to the well-being of our souls. We also need the preaching and teaching of those called by God and authorized by the church. As well, we need the prayers offered in the assembly of the church which Jesus has promised to answer (Matt. 18:19, 20). We need the oversight and accountability provided by church leaders (Heb. 13:17). God is sovereign and may bless His word outside of the church; undoubtedly He has done so. Yet shouldn't our commitment be to that organization and the ordinary means by which He has promised to bless His people?

4

Where Jesus is

We still have not concluded our survey of what Jesus says about the church. Assuredly, some will not be convinced by what we've said about the subject so far. That Jesus said, 'I will build my church' (Matt. 16:18), and says nothing about building anything else, isn't persuasive for them. That He said, 'Tell it to the church' (Matt. 18:17), and intended all that in the way of structure that is implied by that phrase, and all that the Apostles understood by that phrase, still fails to resonate. The keys of the kingdom? The power of binding and loosing? No, some still are not persuaded.

We've saved what is perhaps our strongest argument from Jesus' direct teaching for now. Jesus says in the same Matthew 18 cited above that 'where two or three are gathered in my name, *there am I among them*' (Matt. 18:20). Where is Jesus today? One might assume that because Jesus is God the Son, He is present anywhere and everywhere. Indeed, He is! He is *omni*present. Our interest, however, is not in His *omni presence*, but His *blessed presence*. Granted, that too can be manifested anywhere. We mustn't tie God's hands or restrict Him in any way. He may make His blessed or favorable presence known on the golf course, at the pier, or in my living room.

The serious question for our consideration is, where has He *promised* to be present? The issue is not where He *might* be present but where *will* He be present because He has *promised* to be present? The answer Jesus gives is: in His church, where two or three are gathered in His name. He has promised to be present in the assembly of His disciples, even the most humble of those assemblies. The question then must be: do I wish to be where Jesus is? Dare I miss out on the opportunity to be where Jesus promises to be present? Remember, we've made the case that the church as described in Matthew 18:15-20 cannot be regarded as an informal, *ad hoc*, irregular gathering of self-selecting believers. It has a structure, a membership from which one may be included or excluded; it has standards of belief and conduct to which one must conform, a form of government by which decisions are made, and a system of discipline by which the privileges of membership may be limited or removed.

Where is Jesus? We are given a glimpse of His presence in the post-Ascension church as Christ walks among the seven 'lampstands' which are the seven churches (Rev. 1:20-2:1). Those churches, we may note, are not merely the Christians in a given region, but actual churches that are assessed as collective entities. They are identified as the churches at Ephesus, Smyrna, Pergamum, Thyatira, Sardis, Philadelphia, and Laodicea

(Rev. 2:1–3:22). Repeatedly they are called upon to take collective action in connection with institutional failures. Christ is there, speaking to them, dealing with them on the basis of their collective responsibility. He is present with His assembled church.

What does the presence of the Spirit of Christ among the people of God mean to a believer? Well, everything. Several psalms describe for us, both positively and negatively, what it means to know the *presence* of God among the *people* of God in the *worship* of God. What do they positively say?

> How lovely is your dwelling place,
>   O Lord of hosts!
> My soul longs, yes, faints
>   for the courts of the Lord;
> my heart and flesh sing for joy
>   to the living God (Ps. 84:1-2).

Where God dwells is so 'lovely' that it prompts a yearning in the soul to be present with 'the living God.' 'My soul longs,' he says. 'My soul longs, yes, faints.' For what? 'For the courts of the Lord,' the temple *courts*, God's 'dwelling place.'

> Blessed are those who dwell in your house,
>   ever singing your praise! (Ps. 84:4).

Why would those who 'dwell' in God's 'house' be 'blessed'? Because that is where God is present. That is where His presence is known and felt. This is a thing above all else to be desired.

> For a day in your courts is better
>   than a thousand elsewhere.
> I would rather be a doorkeeper in the house of my God
>   than dwell in the tents of wickedness (Ps. 84:10).

A single day in God's house, enjoying his presence, is better than a thousand days *anywhere* else doing *anything* else. Let that sink in. Nothing in all the world compares with experiencing the presence of God with the people of God in the house of God.

David concurs:

> One thing have I asked of the Lord,
>   that will I seek after:
> that I may dwell in the house of the Lord
>   all the days of my life,
> to gaze upon the beauty of the LORD
>   and to inquire in his temple (Ps. 27:4).

What is the *one thing* that he asks for and seeks? In a world full of comforts and excitements what is his one desire? Simply this: that he may permanently, 'all the days of (his) life,' dwell in the presence of God in the house of God where he might 'gaze upon the beauty of the Lord,' a beauty which is beyond anything else that this world has to offer. In God's presence, David says elsewhere, is 'the fullness of joy' and 'pleasures forevermore' (Ps. 16:11, cf. Pss. 36:8, 73:28, 34:8).

Then, negatively, when excluded or somehow cut off from the presence of God in the house of God with the people of God, the psalmist deeply yearns for restoration.

Psalms 42 and 63 provide two examples. The first of these begins like this:

> As a deer pants for flowing streams,
>   so pants my soul for you, O God.
> My soul thirsts for God,
>   for the living God.
> When shall I come and appear before God?
> (Ps. 42:1-2)

The psalmist is thirsty, yearning for the presence of God like the deer that pants for the water brook. What is going on here? He tells us as he recollects,

> … how I would go with the throng
>   and lead them in procession to the house of God
> with glad shouts and songs of praise,
>   a multitude keeping festival (Ps. 42:4b).

He describes former times when he led a procession of the people of God into the house of God, when in times past his thirst for God was satisfied. Now he longs for that thirst-quenching presence of God. The sister psalm, the 43rd, explains further,

> Send out your light and your truth;
>   let them lead me;
> let them bring me to your holy hill
>   and to your dwelling!
> Then I will go to the altar of God,
>   to God my exceeding joy,
> and I will praise you with the lyre,
>   O God, my God (Ps. 43:3-4).

He longs to be once again at God's 'holy hill,' God's 'dwelling' where he will again enjoy the God who is his '*exceeding* joy.' The greatest of all his joys were those experienced in the presence of God.

We see the same in the 63rd Psalm. David is in the desert wilderness, isolated, alone, cut off from the house of God. The barren landscape of the desert becomes a metaphor for the condition of his soul:

> O God, you are my God; earnestly I seek you;
>   my soul thirsts for you;
> my flesh faints for you,
>   as in a dry and weary land where there is no water
> (Ps. 63:1).

As in the case of Psalm 42, he recalls former times. He *seeks*. He *thirsts*. He *faints*. His soul is in a spiritual desert.

> So I have looked upon you in the sanctuary,
>   beholding your power and glory (Ps. 63:2).

In God's 'sanctuary' he experienced not mere ceremony, not mere ritual, even in the Old Testament era, in which the worship of God was rich in ritual. Rather, he experienced God's 'power and glory' and His 'steadfast love' (*hesed*) which he says is 'better than life,' better than life itself, better than all that life has to offer.

These psalms give us a glimpse of what it means to experience the presence of God among the people of God in the worship of God. So again, we ask, do we wish to be where Jesus promises to be? Can there be any justification for staying home, or 'worshipping' online, or merely listening to sermons? Isn't our physical presence where He is present necessary? Calvin warns, 'Whoever either neglects the sacred assemblies or separates himself from his brethren and is slothful in cultivating unity demonstrates by this fact *that he cares nothing for Christ's presence.*'[1] Do we wish to sit at His feet and be taught? Do we wish to enjoy fellowship with Him (see 1 John 1:1, 2)? Do we wish to experience His presence? Jesus identifies Himself as 'living water' that quenches the thirst of the soul (John 4:14; 7:37). He identifies Himself as the 'bread of life' that satisfies the hunger of the soul (John 6:35). He urges us to come to Him and find rest for our souls (Matt. 11:29). He promises that whoever comes to Him will no longer walk in darkness, but will enjoy the 'light of life' (John 8:12). Where may we experience these blessings of His presence? At church, where two or three have gathered in His name. Again, we cite Calvin: 'The first thing to realize is that *those who desire Christ's presence will meet in His name.*'[2] Where is Jesus? He is wherever His true church is. He is in the midst of the assembly of His people. Is this not where we need to be as well?

---

1. Calvin, *Harmony of the Gospels,* II:232, my emphasis.

2. Ibid., my emphasis.

5

The Good Shepherd and the Sheep

I am the good shepherd. The good shepherd lays down his life for the sheep (John 10:11).

Among the most cherished titles of Christ is that of 'The Good Shepherd.' Never resting, ever vigilant, exposed to the elements, vulnerable to predators, the beloved Shepherd persists in leading, guarding, caring, and providing for His sheep. His sheep? That's us. We are defenseless sheep, creatures capable of neither flight nor fight, prone to wander, easily lost, blindly following, and desperately needing wise shepherding. Jesus provides all that *for us.*

Note the plural noun at the end of the preceding sentence: for *us.* The blessings of the shepherding of the Good Shepherd certainly apply to us *individually.* The Lord is *my* shepherd and consequently, *I* shall not want. He leads *me* to the green pastures. He leads *me* to the still waters. The first person pronoun is prominent right through to the end of the 23rd Psalm: '*I* will dwell in the house of the Lord forever.'

Yet the primary application of the metaphor of the Good Shepherd of John 10 is to us *collectively*, the people of God together. 'Sheep' in English can be either singular or plural. Not so in the original language. The Greek of John 10 is plural. The blessings of the Good Shepherd are promised to God's people collectively. Jesus locates us *together* in the sheepfold (John 10:1-5). He leads us in and out, *together,* to pasture and abundance (John 10:9). There are 'other sheep' who are 'not of this fold,' that is, not of the then current ethnic-national entity the Bible calls Israel that must be brought into the 'fold,' so that there might be 'one flock' under the direction of 'one shepherd.' That 'one flock' is the church into which Israel is transformed:

> And I have other sheep that are not of this fold. I must bring them also, and they will listen to my voice. So there will be one flock, one shepherd (John 10:16).

Sheep, fold, flock: these are all plural entities. The cherished promises of God in connection with the Good Shepherd are given to the people of God collectively, initially Israel, then the church.

Consider this teaching the Gospel of John's equivalent of Matthew 16:18. Jesus is building His church. *The primary application of the Good Shepherd metaphor is to the flock.* The *primary* beneficiary of Jesus' shepherding, His care, His provision, His protection, is the church *collectively,* and me *individually,* in so far as I am a part of the whole. His blessings are realized within the flock as He fends off wolves and thieves (John 10:2,10). His provisions are received by the sheep (plural) as He leads them to pasture and abundance (10:9,10). The 'they' of 'that *they* might have life, and have it abundantly' is plural. The 'abundant' life of the people of God is enjoyed collectively. Our life together is in view.

The application of the 'Good Shepherd' metaphor to which we are driving is obvious. The blessings of the shepherding of the Good Shepherd are found *in the church, along with the other sheep.* That is where safety and provision are to be found. A sheep on its own, separated from the flock, is also separated from the shepherd's care. Such are vulnerable. Such are in mortal danger. Such will not long survive. Likewise, a small group of sheep, wandering off on their own, away from the flock, are exposed to the elements and predators. Sheep belong in the flock, under the care of the Good Shepherd and His pastors, to whom He has entrusted their care (10:1-5). 'Shepherd the *flock* of God' as pastors of the 'chief Shepherd,' the elders are charged (1 Pet. 5:2, 4). 'Pay careful attention … to all the flock, of which the Holy Spirit has made you overseers to care for the *church* of God,' elders again are charged. Life is dangerous enough *inside* of the flock, particularly because of the danger of 'fierce wolves' who, from the outside, 'will *come in among you*, not sparing the *flock*' (Acts 20:28-30). *Outside* the flock is altogether lethal. Only as part of the flock may I have confidence of the protection of the Good Shepherd's rod, and the guidance of His staff.

6

The Apostles and
the Church

Do the Apostles demonstrate an awareness of the implications of Jesus' seminal words regarding the church? Indeed they do. They establish a *structure* for the church and a *dynamic* in the church through which Jesus' intentions might be realized. In both cases, what the Apostles teach reveals the vital role that the church is to play in the life of each believer.

STRUCTURE

'Christ hath instituted a government, and governors ecclesiastical in the church,' declares the Westminster Assembly's *Directory for Church-Government, for Church-Censures, and Ordination of Ministers* (1645).[1] The Apostles, having fulfilled their foundational ministry (Eph. 3:7-10), see to it that elders are appointed for the ongoing life of the church. 'When they had appointed

1. Cited from Wayne R. Spears, 'The Westminster Assembly's Directory for Church Government,' in Charles G. Dennisen and Richard C. Gamble (eds.), *Pressing Toward the Mark: Essays Commemorating Fifty Years of the Orthodox Presbyterian Church* (Philadelphia: The Committee for the History of the Orthodox Presbyterian Church, 1986), 87.

elders for them in every church,' Lystra, Iconium, and Antioch are named, 'they committed them to the Lord' (Acts 14:23). The Apostle Paul addresses the elders of Ephesus (Acts 20:17-38). The elders of Pontus, Galatia, Cappadocia, Asia, and Bithynia are named in connection with the Apostle Peter's self-identification as a 'fellow elder,' as he urges them to 'shepherd the flock of God' (1 Pet.1:1; 5:1-5). The Apostles were succeeded everywhere by councils of elders who were responsible for preserving and promoting the well-being of the church. On the one hand, the churches were 'committed … to the Lord' for *His* safekeeping and care. On the other hand, a crucial step was taken to promote that safekeeping and care: *elders* were appointed.

We find the Apostle Paul's directions to Titus reflecting the same structural commitment as he labors to establish order in the post-apostolic church: 'appoint *elders* in every town as I directed you' (Titus 1:5). Lengthy lists of qualifications for church officers are given in 1 Timothy 3:1-13 and Titus 1:6-9. They must be men of high and tested character because they must 'manage' and 'care for God's church' (1 Tim. 3:5). They 'rule' (1 Tim. 5:17). They have God-given authority. Church members are meant to honor that authority. Listen to the writer to the Hebrews:

> Obey your leaders and submit to them, for they are keeping watch over your souls, as those who will have to give an account. Let them do this with joy and not with groaning, for that would be of no advantage to you (Heb. 13:17).

'Obey,' he says. 'Submit,' he insists. To whom? *Leaders*. The language of authority is unmistakable. They 'lead' (Heb. 13:7). They 'have charge' over members (1 Thess. 5:12, NASB). They exercise 'oversight' (1 Peter 5:2). The reason for this structure, this authority, this government is clear enough: 'They are keeping watch over your souls' (Heb. 13:17). Who are caring for my soul? Leaders are. My individual, spiritual well-being is directly related to my place as a member in the church under the authority of elders. Godly men meeting as a council are to lead the church because this is the best (though not infallible) way to preserve the health of the church and its members.

The church that Jesus intends is at odds with today's climate of hyper-*individualism*. Autonomous, unaccountable, free-floating believers are not envisioned in the New Testament. Detached, uncommitted believers indeed are aloof from the very place meant to provide for their long-term spiritual well-being.

Jesus' church also is at odds with hyper-*collectivism*. Authoritarian, unaccountable, autocratic church leaders cannot sustain the long-term spiritual well-being of believers. Apostles (individuals) replace themselves with elders (groups), not bureaucrats, for the sake of the health and well-being of the churches and their members. They experience this oversight 'not under compulsion' and 'not domineering over those in (their) charge, but being examples to the flock' (1 Pet. 5:2-4). Christian leaders are servant leaders, not 'lord(ing) it over' their people. Yet they do lead, and their people are required to follow

43

(Matt. 20:25-28). The New Testament does not envision believers outside of the visible, institutional church.

DYNAMIC

The church, it must also be said, is more than a structure. It is more than an institution. It is a living organism, a *body*. The Apostles, especially Paul, use this metaphor to teach the mutual dependence, responsibility, and accountability of members for each other. The Apostle Paul develops these thoughts at length in Ephesians 4:11ff, 1 Corinthians 12:4-31 and Romans 12:4-21. The well-being of the church begins with gifted men (pastors and teachers) exercising their word gifts for the equipping of the saints and the building up of the body of Christ (Eph. 4:11-15). This done, each part works properly and the whole body is built up in love (Eph. 4:16). The point receiving emphasis is that the gifts of the Spirit are distributed throughout the whole church body. We are all 'members of one another' (Rom. 12:5). Our gifts are 'for the common good' (1 Cor. 12:7). God has 'arranged the members in the body' and 'composed the body' (1 Cor. 12:18,24). None of us can say to another member, 'I have no need of you,' any more than our eye can say that to our hand or our head to our feet (1 Cor. 12:21). All the parts of the body are 'indispensable' (1 Cor. 12:22).

To which character does John Bunyan give voice to the statement, 'I take my pleasure in walking alone, even more a great deal than in company'? Ignorance. Only the ignorant could think or say such a thing. Only the ignorant would add, as he does, 'unless I like it the better:' that is, the company, he is not interested.[2] Ignorance is a very modern fellow. He prefers a self-selecting fellowship of pilgrims. He'd rather be alone, unless he finds himself among those whose company he likes, according to his own preferences and criteria.

The body metaphor means that I cannot flourish spiritually apart from both the teaching of the gifted pastors and teachers, and a vital, living connection with other believers in the church. My spiritual health, growth, and very survival depend on this connection. The church is a living body in which all 'contribute to the needs of the saints' (Rom. 12:13). We cannot have fingers cut off without being hurt. Fingers cannot sever themselves from the whole body without withering and dying.

What is the church? The church is both an institution and a living organism. The church, as Jesus envisioned it and as the Apostles constructed it, has structure, organization, authority, membership, standards of conduct and belief, discipline, means of inclusion and exclusion, officers, a Great Commission, ministry and sacraments. It is also a living, growing, diverse body of mutually dependent parts. We repeat: the New Testament does not envision a believer outside of the church. Those who believe are baptized, the church's rite of admission, and they are 'added to the number,' the roll, of the church (Acts 2:38, 47; 4:4). Is not 'in the church' where Jesus wants us, and where we need to be?

---

2. See John Bunyan, *Pilgrim's Progress* (1678; 1895; Edinburgh; The Banner of Truth Trust, 1977), 166.

7
Body and Head, Bride and Groom

Still not convinced of the central role that the church is to play in a believer's life and commitments? Let's continue to develop the nature of Jesus' relationship to the church as expressed by the metaphors employed by the Apostles. As we've seen, two of their favorites are the church as the 'body of Christ' (1 Cor. 12:12-31; Rom. 12:4-8; Eph. 4:11ff) and as 'the bride of Christ' (Ps. 45; Song of Solomon; 2 Cor. 11:2; Rev. 21:2, 9; 19:7, 9). Is it possible to harmonize these metaphors of the church with the philosophy of churchless Christianity? Can we claim a healthy relationship with Jesus while rejecting His body and bride?

BODY AND HEAD
So far we have considered the 'body' only in terms of the relationship of the parts or members of the body to each other. More importantly, what is the relationship between the parts and the head? Can the body be severed from the head and the body still survive? 'Christ is the head of the church, his body' (Eph. 5:23). Of course

not. Can one be separated from the body and still be connected to the head? Again, of course not. Believers must remain in union with the body in order to be in vital union with Christ their head (See John 15:1-5). Further, can one love the head and despise the body? Of course, that too is impossible. The head and the body are one, distinguishable but inseparable. Ordinarily, we love or hate whole persons. We don't love their head and hate their body, or the reverse. This particularly is true since (according to this metaphor) we are part of that body. No one ever hates his own body, says the Apostle, 'but nourishes and cherishes it, just as Christ does the church, because we are members of his body' (Eph. 5:29, 30). 'My love to myself is hot,' admits the Puritan George Swinnock (1627-1673) as he develops the metaphor of the body along these lines in his classic, 'The Christian Man's Calling.' Of course it is. We love ourselves.

> How *tender* I am of myself under any malady! How *pitiful* towards myself in any misery! How *patient* toward myself when I discover many infirmities! My love to myself is *hearty*.[1]

If this is how I view myself, then this also must be how I love the church: tenderly, full of pity, patiently, vigorously. I love the head, Christ, so also must I love the body of which I am a part. It may be ill or injured; it may be confused or erring, yet I must love it.

---

1. George Swinnock, 'Christian Man's Calling,' in *The Works of George Swinnock*, Vol. 1 (1868; Edinburgh: The Banner of Truth Trust, 1992), I:500 (my emphasis).

BRIDE OF CHRIST

Second, let's consider applying the biblical metaphor of the church as bride to churchless Christianity. *Jesus loves His bride-wife.* He shed His blood for her. He nourishes and cherishes her (Eph. 5:25-33). Can one love Christ and despise His bride-wife? Can one separate Christ from His beloved? Can one love Him and ignore her? Imagine inviting a friend for dinner and urging him to leave his wife at home because, as you explain, you like him, not her; you are interested in getting to know him better but can't be bothered about her. A friendship with the husband is not sustainable under these conditions.

Remember *we* are His bride-wife. We have been loved by our husband-groom with the purity and intensity of a groom's love for his bride. 'Behold, you are beautiful, my love; behold you are beautiful,' Christ says to us through the voice of the groom (Song 1:15; 4:1). 'You are altogether beautiful, my love; there is no flaw in you.' 'How much better is your love than wine … my dove, my perfect one' (Song 4:1, 10; 6:9). Heaven's celebration culminates in 'the marriage supper of the Lamb,' as Christ's bride, the church is brought to Him. The 'new Jerusalem' descends from heaven from God, 'prepared as a bride adorned for her husband' (Rev. 19:7-9; 21:2).

Swinnock encourages us to ponder the magnitude of Christ's love for His bride-church, drawing from Ephesians 5:22ff and 1 Peter 2:4-11. 'My Saviour's love is chaste … constant … fervent … perpetual … pure,' he exclaims. Follow his adverbs:

> Oh how *industriously* did my Redeemer endeavor his church's renovation and sanctity! how *affectionately* doth he beseech her to be holy! how *fervently* doth he beg of his Father to make her holy! how *willingly* did he broach his heart, and pour out his blood to wash her from her unholiness! how *plentifully* doth he pour down his Spirit to work her to holiness![2]

The whole life and ministry of Christ was prompted by love for His bride-church:

> His *birth* was that she might be born again, and born holy. His *life* was to set her a copy of holiness; his *death* was to purchase for her a new stock of holiness. He 'gave himself for her, that he might redeem her from all iniquity, and purify unto himself a peculiar people, zealous of good works.' His precepts, his prayers, his tears, his blood, his birth, his life, his death, his resurrection, his intercession, are *all for her holiness and purity.*[3]

The church is both Christ's body and His bride. Both metaphors indicate the most intimate care, concern, interest, and love. How can we not respond to His love with our own love for that which He loves, His church? 'He who does not heartily love the church,' says another Puritan, George Hamond (1620-1705), 'does not sincerely love Christ Himself.'[4]

---

2. Swinnock, 'Christian Man's Calling,' in *Works,* I:499, 500, citing 1 Peter 2:4-11 (my emphasis).

3. Ibid., 500 (my emphasis).

4. George Hamond, *The Case for Family Worship* (1694; Orlando: Soli Deo Gloria, 2005), 106.

8

One Anothers and Community

A new commandment I give to you, that you love
one another: just as I have loved you, you also are to
love one another. By this all people will know that
you are my disciples, if you have love for one another
(John 13:34, 35).

Walk in. Walk out. That sums up the relationship that
some people have with their churches. They walk in at
10:59 am. They sit quietly for the service. They walk
out at 12:05 pm. That is it. Their participation in the
life and ministry of the church goes no further. Aside
from a perfunctory 'Good morning' and maybe a 'Fine,
thank you' or 'I'm good' answering another's 'How are
you today?' no more interaction occurs. In they come.
Out they go.

IDEAL

The reluctant practice of our church is to leave alone
our members and visitors who settle for this level
of participation. We caution newcomers that our

51

congregation will not feel like home unless they are also involved in either Sunday School or the evening service and meal, or best of all, both. If, over time, we see that they are content with a Sunday morning only level of participation, we leave them undisturbed. We worry about them eventually moving to a church down the street with the predictable 'we just never felt like we fit in,' or 'we tried to break in but never could.' Yet, if they are content, we don't continue to badger them with pleas to get more involved.

Still, this level of participation is not the biblical ideal. How do we know? The quick answer is the 'one anothers.' By my count there are twenty-eight of them, some of which are particularly featured in the passages we just reviewed (Rom. 12, 1 Cor. 12, Eph. 4:11ff). They paint a picture of what our church life is supposed to look like. They tell us a great deal about our relationships in the church, beginning with Jesus' new commandment that we 'love one another' (John 13:34, 35). Jesus provides us with perspective on how we are to relate to our fellow members. 'Love, just as I have loved you' tells us all that we need to know about the depth and breadth of our commitment to each other. 'By this will all men know that you are my disciples' tells us of the vital connection between our mutual love and our mission. No wonder 'love one another' is repeated eleven more times in the New Testament (John 15:12, 17; Rom. 13:8; 1 Thess. 3:12, 4:9; 1 Pet. 1:22; 1 John 3:11, 23; 4:7, 11, 21).

The other twenty-seven 'one anothers' flesh out what that love looks like. We are to care for (1 Cor. 12:25), serve (Gal. 5:13), be kind and tenderhearted (Eph. 4:32), forgive (Eph. 4:32; Col. 3:13), comfort (1 Thess. 4:18), show hospitality (1 Pet. 4:9), teach and admonish (Col. 3:16), be devoted and show preference to one another (Rom. 12:9,10), and so on. A high level of *commitment to* and *involvement in* each other's lives is envisioned, is it not? If 'love one another' is the most comprehensive of the 'one anothers,' perhaps 'bear one another's burdens' is the most concrete (Gal. 6:2). Together, the 'one anothers' provide a picture of our duties and responsibilities as members of the church. Take them away and a giant hole results in the New Testament picture of what it means to live a Christian life. Eliminate the 'one anothers' and a huge chunk of the Christian life simply disappears.

CRUCIAL LESSON

Perhaps the first lesson to be drawn from the 'one anothers' is that of realizing my evaluation of the church in the first instance is 'not about me,' as the expression goes, or at least it should not be. My first question when assessing my experience of the church should not be 'what am I getting out of it?' or 'are my needs being met?'

Not that these are irrelevant questions. It is valid to question if a church is doing all that it should be doing or at least enough of what it could be doing to merit our loyalty. For example, if God's gospel-word is not being preached, undoubtedly one's needs are *not* being met. Also, if a church's services do not feature substantial prayer, or congregational singing, or sufficient Bible reading, or regular administration of the sacraments, one will not 'get out of it' what God intends that we get out of the congregation's weekly assemblies. It would be odd if our souls did not languish in the absence of one or more of these central elements of a properly-constituted worship service.

Still, the primary lesson of the 'one anothers' is that my first question about my church should not be about what I am *getting* but what I am *giving*. Am I loving the brethren? Am I devoted to the flock? Am I bearing the brethren's burdens? My experience of the life of the church unavoidably will be unsatisfactory if I am focused on whether I am *being served* adequately, rather than whether I am *serving* adequately.

My consistent observation over thirty years of pastoral ministry is that those who throw themselves into the life of the church, attending services, eager to serve, wanting to be involved, hungry for fellowship, are received warmly by current members and immediately begin to thrive. They quickly establish deep and lasting friendships. At the same time, those who remain uninvolved or under-involved, who are distant and detached from the vital heart of the church's ministry, never do 'fit in.' They grow discontent. They fail to make connections with others. They may perceive inadequacies in the structure of our church life. They may observe from the sidelines what we lack, offering suggestions for improvement. They may even conclude there is not enough love in the church, or care, or fellowship, not grasping at all the irony of this self-imposed context of isolation and discontent.

PERSONAL EVALUATION

'Community' is one of the buzz-words of our day. Many people, especially among the young, are in search of rich community life. The 'one anothers' reveal that without *commitment*, there can be no *community*.

Undoubtedly there are many deficiencies in our church and in every church. It would be arrogant for us to deny this. Of course, some churches fail in many areas and all churches fail in some areas. Often, our critics help us to see where and how to improve our ministry and we can be grateful to them. Yet consideration of the implications of the 'one anothers' should lead to deeper personal self-evaluation. Does my commitment to the church resemble the level of participation indicated by the 'one anothers'? Does my Christian life match the portrait painted by the 'one anothers' in the New Testament? Furthermore, does my discontent (if there is such) result not from any inadequacies in the church itself, but from the inadequacies of my commitment to its ministry and members, hence, to community, and ultimately to Christ Himself?

9
Church Membership

At this point some may concede our argument that the church is important, even that the church is an institution to which we are to be committed. Yet they may still insist that they don't see church membership in the Bible. 'Membership is man's invention, not God's,' they may claim. They may point to the number of highly successful churches, even mega-churches, that have no official membership at all.

Our answer is membership is exactly what we see in Scripture from Abraham to the Apostles, from Genesis to Revelation. The people of God throughout the Bible form a covenant community. They covenant together. They make promises to God and to each other to be God's faithful and obedient people. This has always been the case.

THE OLD TESTAMENT

God's covenant is made with Abraham and his 'offspring … throughout the generations' (Gen. 17:7, 10, 19). God Himself explains,

> For I have chosen him, that he may command his children and his household after him to keep the way of the LORD by doing righteousness and justice, so that the LORD may bring to Abraham what he has promised him (Gen. 18:19).

Covenant promises and obligations are passed along to 'his household and his household after him,' to Isaac (Gen. 26:3-5, 24), to Jacob (Gen. 28:3, 4, 14; 35:9-12), and to Jacob's sons (Gen. 48-49). They grow into tribes, and the tribes into a nation which covenants together under Moses to keep the Passover (Exod. 12, 13) and obey all the laws of God. Upon the verge of Jordan, after hearing the blessings and curses of the covenant, they renew the covenant with God together (Deut. 27-30). Most dramatically, upon the conquest of the land of promise, Joshua charges the people together:

> Now therefore fear the LORD and serve him in sincerity and in faithfulness. Put away the gods that your fathers served beyond the River and in Egypt, and serve the LORD. And if it is evil in your eyes to serve the LORD, choose this day whom you will serve, whether the gods your fathers served in the region beyond the River, or the gods of the Amorites in whose land you dwell. But as for me and my house, we will serve the LORD (Josh 24:14, 15).

The people respond, 'We also will serve the Lord, for he is our God' (Josh. 24:18). So it is throughout the Old Testament historical narratives, Genesis to Nehemiah, the prophets, Isaiah to Malachi rightly being understood as prosecutors of the covenant, calling the people of God back to their covenantal obligations to God and to each other.

We even see something like membership rolls in the Old Testament. Hence, we find a number of long lists of names and numbers of those participating in covenantal activity. A census is taken at Sinai in Numbers 1–2 (see authorization: Exod. 30:11-16; 38:26), and again prior to the conquest of Canaan (Num. 26:1-65). Genealogical records are found in 1 Chronicles 1-9 leading into David's reign. The precise number of exiles returning from Babylon is recorded in Ezra 2 and Nehemiah 7:6-67). The names of those rebuilding the walls of Jerusalem are found in Nehemiah 3.

THE NEW TESTAMENT

We come to the New Testament and Jesus expressly establishes a 'new covenant' in His blood, instituting the covenantal meal of that new covenant community (Matt. 26:28; Mark 14:24; Luke 22:20). This 'Lord's Supper,' like Passover, ratifies and confirms or reaffirms covenant commitments, both God's and His people's. The people of God make promises to God *or to each other*. The essential characteristics of the covenant continue. Continuity between the Old Testament and the New Testament is assumed, which is why the Apostle Paul can refer to baptism, the New Testament rite of admission as 'the circumcision of Christ,' referring to the Old Testament rite of admission (Col. 2:11, 12).

The point: the covenant community is one in which members are bound together by oaths, by promises to God and to each other. The result: they are able to rely on each other. They can count on each other. They will be there for each other. They are responsible for each other. Those who gather informally and periodically with a self-selecting group of fellow believers have no concrete commitments. When they walk out of the coffee shop, they may also walk out of each other's lives, permanently. The informal pattern of fellowship implies no particular obligations and provides no actual security. This, however, is not the nature of the relationship between believers as envisioned by the New Testament, as we saw when we looked at the 'one anothers.'

Marriage vows are viewed by some as superfluous. What matters is love, they say. As long as two people love each other, they may live together and enjoy all of the benefits of marriage without the commitments of marriage. Our view is this arrangement offers no security to either partner. When feelings or opportunities change, one's loved one may head for the exit, leaving emotional devastation in his or her wake. Marriage vows matter. They provide security. They define the nature of the commitment being made. The traditional vows obligate a life-long commitment. That is a different kind of commitment than one which merely obligates 'as long as we both shall *love*.' The man and woman in the traditional vows are promising to be there for each other 'for better for worse; in plenty and in want; in joy and in sorrow; in sickness and in health.' Whatever comes in life, I will be there for you. You can depend on me.

So it is with church membership. We vow, barring providential hindrances, to be there for each other. We bind ourselves together in a relationship of mutual support and mutual accountability. Pressing the marriage analogy, we are a family, brothers and sisters, devoted to each other, bearing each other's burdens, preferring each other, and loving each other, not as it is convenient to do so, not so long as I benefit, but 'for better for worse, as long as we both shall live.'

10
Life Together: A Case Study

A recent review article in a Christian periodical makes the claim that 'an hour or a few given to Christian worship in a week is not sufficient to form the primary loves and desires of people who are being formed in rival and often contrary loves the rest of the week.'[1] The author argues that the whole structure of the church's life plays a vital role in counteracting the impact of the culture throughout the week. That got me thinking about the value of a regular weekly and annual routine in the life of the church. We may use the program of the Independent Presbyterian Church as a case study, a window as it were, through which to view how the pattern of church life builds commitment and community.

ANNUAL PATTERN
Each summer, our congregation worships Sunday nights from Memorial Day weekend (last Sunday in May) to Labor Day weekend (first Sunday in September) at our

---

1. Jason Micheli, 'Can Christians Transform Culture?' in *The Christian Century*, August 29, 2018, Vol. 135, No. 18, p. 34.

Point Pleasant camp facility. This tradition predates my arrival in Savannah thirty plus years ago. Certain 'rituals' tie these summers together. We begin and end each summer with informal singing for the fifteen minutes before the service begins, culminating in singing the contemporary version of Psalm 134:

> Behold, Bless the Lord, all children of the LORD,
> Who stand by night in the house of the LORD.
> Lift up your hands to the sanctuary,
> And bless the LORD.

Following announcements, we begin the service itself, a traditional Presbyterian order featuring the Word read (a chapter), preached (exposition), sung (Psalms and hymns), prayed (a full diet of biblical prayer) and displayed (in the sacraments). A 'Church-Wide Barbecue' follows the service in May; a 'Low Country Boil' in September. The actual services at the opening and closing of the summer at Point Pleasant each conclude with the singing of 'When Peace like a River', with its two-part refrain. Repetition of these songs each year stirs up memories of worship services and Christian fellowship going back decades. We recall our child-rearing years and our children growing into adults. Now, we look across the room at our grandchildren. Our children themselves recall the singing, the food, playing in the marsh, and hunting for fiddler crabs.

My point is: these are powerful builders of community. They help mark our identity as a congregation. The songs, the meals, the families in fellowship: this is what we do each summer. This is who we are: summer nights at Point Pleasant, singing 'Behold, bless the Lord" (Psalm 134) and 'It is Well with My Soul;' enjoying a church-wide barbecue in the spring and a low-country boil in the fall

The same is true of Easter. Easter week, we conduct a service of 'Lessons and Psalms.' All the 'Passion narratives' from the four gospels are read. The psalms associated with these narratives are sung (e.g. Pss. 16, 22, 35, 41, 69, 110, 118, etc.). The impact of this extended meditation upon Christ's suffering is powerful. Easter Saturday, we have a pancake breakfast at Point Pleasant. Easter Sunday, we open our Easter service with 'Christ the Lord is Risen Today.' The church is full. The first audible notes from the congregation are startlingly loud. The singing is powerfully moving. Each year, we conclude the morning service with Handel's 'Hallelujah Chorus.' Each year, we are overcome with emotion at the sheer beauty and majesty of it all.

As summer ends, we conduct an annual 'Communion Season' with services Thursday – Saturday, culminating in Sunday communion. We read the great gospel texts. We sing the great evangelical hymns: 'When I Survey the Wondrous Cross;' 'Alas! and Did My Savior Bleed;' 'O Sacred Head, Now Wounded;' and 'O the Deep, Deep Love of Jesus.' The daily services culminate when we gather at the table, the elements representing Christ and His benefits, and the deep bonds of commitment and conviction that we share.

Each fall, we host a 'Fall Family Night' on October 31 as an alternative to the pagan and occultic observance of

Halloween. We organize rides and games for the children, with food and candy for everyone. The neighborhood joins us. Costumes are donned and fun is had by all. This is a staple of our congregational life.

Each Christmas season, we have a 'Service of Lessons and Carols' followed by a Christmas buffet. This has been the tradition for over thirty years. The sanctuary is beautifully decorated. The singing is gorgeous. The food is delicious. The fondest of memories are associated with this event. The Christmas Eve service provides more of the same. Every year, we open the service with 'O Come All Ye Faithful.' Many of us struggle to choke out the words. Every year, we close with 'Joy to the World.' We exit the building and sing a series of carols on the lawn by candlelight. No one wants to miss that service. It is our tradition. It is what we do. It is who we are. It is a staple of our congregational life.

Each winter/spring, we conduct a 'Mission's Conference,' Thursday through Sunday, the Sunday morning service beginning with Isaac Watt's great paraphrase of Psalm 72, 'Jesus Shall Reign,' and we hear challenging messages from missionaries and guest preachers.

We are not a calendar-driven church. Philosophically, we are opposed to the full 'church calendar' of Advent, Lent, and so on. We limit ourselves to the 'five evangelical feast days' of Christmas, Good Friday (Maundy Thursday), Easter, Ascension, and Pentecost. Even then, we treat the latter two with a light touch. Yet we can see that there is an important, identity-forming role played by the annual cycle in the church's life. The world has its calendar; we combat it with ours.

WEEKLY PATTERN

More importantly, our weekly services forge our identity as a community, shaping our understanding of who we are, what we believe, and what we do. We have had for generations a weekly routine, a weekly tradition of 9:30 Sunday School, followed by 11:00 morning worship and 5:30 evening service. We sing two hymns and a psalm in our services. Singing a classic hymn at Independent Presbyterian Church such as, 'Holy, Holy, Holy,' or 'Praise to the Lord the Almighty,' or 'Be Thou My Vision,' or any one of literally dozens of other hymns and psalms is a powerful experience for our people. We read a lengthy passage of Scripture. We recite the Creed and the Lord's Prayer. We pray and preach. We observe not weekly, but monthly Communion. Week in, week out, fifty-two weeks a year, morning and evening, this is what we do. This is who we are.

Remarkably, our people grow to love traditional hymnody and metrical psalmody. If they move to other communities, they miss 'the music.' They long to sing the substantial hymns and biblical psalms and the tunes of enduring quality. When visiting other churches, they notice the absence of extended Scripture reading and miss it. They notice the absence of serious prayer and feel a void as a result. They observe the less-than-rigorous attention to the text of Scripture in the preaching and yearn for truly biblical exposition. Their identity, their convictions, their commitment, their desires have been forged by our routines and traditions.

COMMITMENT

Commitment to a church means commitment to its program and its people. Those who commit to its program, who are there each week for each service all through the year, grow to love the weekly and annual routine. They grow to love the regular services and the special services. They are *moved* by the routines and traditions that mark who we are and what we do.

Because they are committed to the program of the church, they become committed to the people. This commitment follows naturally and organically because *they are there* at the church *among its people*. They are present at services, mingling with the members before and after. They are present for the coffee and sweets before Sunday School and morning service, getting to know others through casual conversation. They stay for the evening meal, sitting across the table from other members over an extended period of time, deepening the bonds of fellowship with them. Their children are becoming the best friends of the other children of the church. Common convictions with a common outlook and common priorities are forged. A community of like-minded people emerges who love each other, care for each other, and bear each other's burdens. Through regular involvement in the program of the church, their hearts are knit together. It happens subtly, slowly, unperceptively. Often, we fail to recognize how wonderful and beautiful it all is, until sadly, perhaps by death or by relocation, it ends.

The building of congregational identity is aided when the pattern of church life extends beyond one's local church. If one is part of a national denomination in which there is substantial unity in worship, it helps. Of course, from place to place, there will be variations in details. Not every church has a Point Pleasant. Not every church has an organ. Not every church sets up tables down the center aisle for communion. Yet if, when one relocates to a new community, or one goes on vacation, one can find a sister church which features morning and evening worship, expository preaching, substantial Bible reading, a full diet of biblical prayer, and traditional psalmody/hymnody, one may find oneself happily 'at home.' One may even realize, 'There are lots of us. We are not alone.' The Episcopalians seem to know who they are and what they'll get when they walk through the doors of an Episcopal church: Prayer Book worship. Regrettably, maybe fatally, the days of liturgical unity are long gone among conservative Presbyterians, unlikely to return.

The world's 'liturgies' are pervasive and powerful. Its calendar of events, from Super Bowl, to pop concert, to three-day weekend, to the Easter bunny, to Halloween, to Santa Claus; its music, its literature, its arts, its use of media, its accepted 'truths,' its received 'values,' all conspire to undermine Christian faith. The world's calendar all but smothers ours. The church is organized in opposition to the world and the world returns the favor. The church eventually will not only conquer the world, but batter down hell's gates as well. Yet we will only see it do so in our time and place if we are committed to the church's program, if we are active participants in our 'life together.'

11

Covenant and Care

So then, as we have opportunity, let us do good to
everyone, and especially to those who are of the
household of faith (Gal. 6:10).

Can one be too committed to the church? The question
is raised by those who fear we may become committed
to our church to the exclusion of other believers and
friendship with unbelievers. Are we in danger of
becoming a Christian ghetto? Aloof from outsiders,
isolated from unbelievers, cloistered to the point of
irrelevance? This is not an unimportant question,
especially if considered historically. Variations on
the monastic impulse have appeared and reappeared
throughout the centuries. From hermit monks, to
communal monks, to Benedict, to the Cistercians, to
the Jesuits, to the Anabaptists – such as the Mennonites
and Amish – to the fundamentalists of the early
twentieth century, separation from the world has been
both a temptation and a strategy for Christians.

IN, NOT OF, THE WORLD

The old formula is a good one: be *in* the world, not *of* the world. Jesus commands us to be light and salt *in the world* of darkness and corruption. We are to be 'a city set on a hill' that cannot be hidden (Matt. 5:13, 14). Jesus commands,

> Let your light shine before others, so that they may see your good works and give glory to your Father who is in heaven (Matt. 5:16).

Our light is to shine 'before others' who are able to 'see (our) good works' with the salutary result of God's glory. Similarly, the Apostle Paul, undoubtedly echoing Jesus' teaching, instructs us to be

> … blameless and innocent, children of God without blemish in the midst of a crooked and twisted generation, among whom you shine as lights in the world, holding fast to the word of life (Phil. 2:15-16a).

Note where he places us: '*in the midst* of a crooked and twisted generation,' yet 'as lights *in the world.*' Elsewhere, he intends that we *should* 'associate' with the 'sexually immoral of this world … the greedy and swindlers' and 'idolaters,' since, to avoid them, we 'would need to go out of this world,' a thing not to be done (1 Cor. 5:9, 10). It is only when such evil-doers claim to be Christian brethren that we are not to 'associate' with them, 'not even to eat with such a one' (1 Cor. 5:11; also 2 Thess. 3:6,14; 2 Tim. 3:5; 2 John 10). Clearly, the implication is that we would have significant relationships with worldlings. We are to be *in the world*.

On the other hand, we are not to be *of the world*. Hence, in Jesus' 'High Priestly Prayer,' He prays, 'I do not ask that you take them out of the world,' but that we be protected 'from the evil one' (John 17:15). Indeed, 'I have sent them *into the world*' (John 17:18), yet 'the world has hated them because they are not of the world just as I am *not of the world*' (John 17:14). Again,

> They are not of the world, just as I am not of the world (John 17:16).

We are to remain separate from the world and its ways. We are to 'love not the world or the things of the world' (1 John 2:15). 'Friendship with the world' is forbidden (James 4:4). Most emphatically, the Apostle Paul urges, 'Do not be unequally yoked with unbelievers' (2 Cor. 6:14a). He then asks,

> For what partnership has righteousness with lawlessness? Or what fellowship has light with darkness? What accord has Christ with Belial? Or what portion does a believer share with an unbeliever? What agreement has the temple of God with idols? (2 Cor. 14b-16a).

He then cites Leviticus 26:12, commanding us,

> Therefore go out from their midst, and be separate from them, says the Lord, and touch no unclean thing (2 Cor. 6:17; cf. Rev. 18:4, 5).

Covenantal priority

How do we put these two strands of being *in* the world but not *of* the world together? We do so by establishing a covenantal priority. Our first and primary obligation is to our Christian brothers and sisters, to whom we are bound by covenant vows. We are part of the same family, not by birth, but by covenant. This priority is perhaps most clearly expressed by the Apostle Paul in Galatians 6:10.

> So then, as we have opportunity, let us do good to everyone, and especially to those who are of the household of faith (Gal. 6:10).

We are to aim to 'do good to everyone,' believer and non-believer. It would be ridiculous for us to reject an opportunity to help an unbeliever by saying, 'Sorry, you are not a part of my group.' Of course we 'do good' wherever and whenever and with whomever we can. Yet the priority is 'the household of faith.' They 'especially' are the objects of our love and care. For example, the charitable, diaconal ministry of the church does not aim to alleviate all human suffering, but suffering within the church. The widow who receives the care of the church is the Christian widow, and not just any Christian widow, but one 'having been *the wife of one husband, and having a reputation for good works: if she has brought up children, has shown hospitality, has washed the feet of the saints, has cared for the afflicted, and has devoted herself to every good work*' (1 Tim. 5:9b-10). That is a pretty high bar for being on the receiving end of diaconal help. The priority for believers is the faithful within the covenant community.

The 'one anothers' of our previous study also are directed to members of churches (e.g. Rome, Ephesus, Colossae, Corinth, Galatia, etc.) regarding *their fellow members*. Sometimes, they explicitly are directed to give to believers and churches outside their congregations; one example is when the Apostle Paul urges the Corinthians to give generously to the needy Jerusalem church, as the churches of Macedonia (e.g. Philippi) had done (e.g. 2 Cor. 8-9; cf. Rom. 15:25-28; 1 Cor. 16:1-4). However, this is the exception that proves the rule. Unless otherwise indicated, the Apostles are directing us (in their twenty-eight 'one anothers') to love, care for, and bear the burdens of our fellow church members. It is not that we are to withhold care and kindness from other believers or unbelievers; again, we should be Good Samaritans to everyone with whom we come into contact. Rather, we are being guided in establishing priorities and ordering our commitments accordingly.

Can we be too committed to the church? Yes, if it means that we are either isolated from outsiders or withhold kindness from them. Yet frankly, I've not been aware of this as a significant problem. Indeed, I don't recall seeing anyone in the last thirty years who was too committed to the church. No one. On the other hand, I've seen lots of believers compromised by love of the world. I've seen lots of believers failing to 'love one another' because all of their energies are poured into their 'friends,' from whom they derive social satisfaction and benefit. I've seen lots of believers who are (typically, to be honest) worldly Christians or outright worldlings. Our priority, that which ought to receive the benefit of our thoughts, time, energy, and love, should be the young and the old, the rich and the poor, the Jew and the Gentile, the hip and the unhip, the cool and the uncool, the connected and the unconnected of our own church home, and then of the broader Christian community. Our priorities in dispensing care are ordered by God's covenant with us in Christ.

III
Clarifying Perspectives

12
Church or Christians?

Not infrequently, believers are talking past each other as they discuss the church and the various responsibilities of believers. We can speak of 'definitional confusion.' When the word 'church' is uttered, what exactly is meant? Some people mean a church service ('Are you going to *church* tomorrow?'), others a church building ('What a beautiful *church!*'), still others Christianity generally ('What can we learn from *church* history?'), just to cite the most obvious examples. We will want to focus on several of these, hoping that, by doing so, we may bring clarity to our discussion.

We may begin with the loose use of the terms 'church' and 'Christian.' Popularly, they are used interchangeably, which contributes considerably to the confusion surrounding today's discussions of the church. While they have overlapping content, they are not coextensive. There are things which are true of individual Christians, which may not be true of the church. So also the reverse. There are things that are true of the church that are not true of the individual. Yet sometimes, we speak of 'the church' when we mean individual Christians or informal groups of Christians. Sometimes we speak of 'Christians' when we actually mean the church. Two areas in which this confusion is particularly damaging are those of culture and commitment. Let me explain.

CULTURE

Sincere but disillusioned Christians may say, 'The *church* needs to be doing more about _____' or 'The *church* has failed by its neglect to do anything or say anything about _____.' The blanks are filled with important social and cultural issues: education, poverty, racism, employment, moral controversies, abortion, etc., about which the church is perceived as having been negligent. 'Aren't Christians supposed to be involved in culture, social issues, and politics?' they ask. Christians are. That is the point. *Christians* are; the *church* may or may not. A few years ago my denomination's General Assembly featured the motto, 'Anchored in Christ, Active in Culture.' Unanswered was the question, 'Who is?' Is the motto addressed to the church as the church or to the church as individuals or groups of Christians? Since it was a gathering of the church as the church, I assumed the former, which meant discomfort on my part with the motto.

The church as an institution has a fairly narrow job description. Essentially it is this: worship and witness. The Great Commission, its job description, has us making disciples of the nations, baptizing them into the fellowship of the church, and teaching them all that Jesus commands (Matt. 28:19-20; Mark 16:15-16; Luke 24:47-49; John 20:21-23). The New Testament portrays the early Christians gathering for simple services of teaching, prayer, the Lord's Supper, and fellowship (Acts 2:42; 1 Tim. 2:1, 2; 4:13). We do not find any direct attempts to fight Roman political oppression, abolish slavery, end social inequality, or relieve poverty. The church is competent to gather for worship and evangelize and make disciples. It has done an admirable job of this for 2,000 years. However, once it strays from these simple tasks it quickly reveals its incompetence while at the same time it neglects the very work that it was commissioned to do.

Years ago a political cartoon showed a clergyman at a chalkboard drawing up the X's and O's of a football play. Arrows showed the players moving wildly in every direction. As a football play, it was senseless. The caption was, 'The bishop's statement on the economy.' The point was clear enough, even if the chalkboard was incoherent. When it comes to the economy, the editorial page cartoonist was convinced that the church doesn't know what it is talking about. 'Active in culture' is not what the church is called to be. It is active in being a counter-culture by its proclamation of 'sin, righteousness, and the judgment to come' (John 16:8), by the quality of its sacrificial love and by its high moral standards. It is called to relieve poverty (2 Cor. 8, 9), to end bigotry and prejudice (Gal. 2:11-14; 3:28), to treat others impartially and without regard to social status (James 2:1-7) *among its own.* However, the church as an institution has no particular social mission outside its walls, out there *in the culture.*

At the same time, individuals and groups of individual Christians *are* called to all manner of social and cultural activity. Some are called to artistic excellence. Others are called to literary excellence. Still others to scientific excellence. Christians are called to the full spectrum of worldly activities. Some are called to be politicians or professionals (not just politicians or professionals who happen to be Christians, but politicians or professionals who think and act like Christians). Others, similarly, are called to be Christian athletes or laborers. Still others are called to be Christian craftsmen or homemakers. As Christians pursue their vocations in the world, they bring light and salt into the community; they bring reform and reformation. So it was that Christians, such as member of Parliament William Wilberforce (1759-1833) and other members of a voluntary organization known as the 'Clapham Sect,' successfully led the movement for the abolition of slavery in the British Empire.[1] Christians have established schools, colleges and universities, including nearly every private institution for higher education in the United States until the late 1800s. They have been patrons of the arts. They have established hospitals and countless organizations to help the poor, workers, immigrants, widows and orphans. They have formed all manner of charitable organizations and

---

1. See E. M. Howse, *Saints in Politics: The 'Clapham Sect' and the Growth of Freedom* (Toronto: University of Toronto Press, 1952).

reform movements to combat social evils and promote social well-being.

This distinction between what Christians are supposed to do (the list of which may be limitless) and what the church is supposed to do (which is limited and particular) is crucial. It frees Christians to pursue their callings across the entire range of normal human activities, and it saves the church from false accusations, unwarranted expectations, dissipated energies, and mission creep.

COMMITMENT

The second area where this confusion of church/Christian terminology persists is in the realm of commitment. 'I'm committed to the church,' many sincere believers maintain, while remaining uncommitted to a particular church. What they mean is, 'I'm committed to the group of Christians with whom I associate.' We don't need to labor the point because we've discussed this problem at length already. We seek only briefly to remind ourselves that a group that gets together monthly in its members' living room, or weekly in a restaurant, or Sundays in a coffee shop, that is voluntary, *ad hoc*, informal, self-selecting, and affinity-driven is not the church. It *is* a group of Christians. One might be committed at some level or even a serious level to a group of fellow believers who have gathered around a particular interest or affinity. Yet such groups of Christians are not the church. Identifying them as such is confusing things that differ. It betrays definitional confusion. The church, as we have seen, is an institution, an organization, and, as such, calls for my commitment to it and my support of it.

I may or may not be committed to meeting with my circle of Christian friends. That is my choice. There are no commandments, instructions, or directions about such meetings or gatherings. Not so the church. Gathering with the church that Jesus is building, that has a government, officers, membership, a method of discipline, and standards of inclusion and exclusion is *an obligatory commitment for all believers* (Matt. 16:18; 18:15-20). Support and participation are not considered voluntary. Believers are not permitted to 'neglect' (ESV) or 'forsake' the assembly (Heb. 10:25, NASB). Non-commitment is a non-option. Commitment to the church as the church, not the 'church' as a self-selecting group of believers, is a necessary part of what it means to be a Christian.

13
Visible or Invisible?

A second area of definitional confusion has to do with the visibility and invisibility of the church. Behind the diminished regard for the church today is an overblown doctrine of the church's invisibility. Quite often, quite unwittingly, the word 'church' itself has been defined differently by its users depending upon the context. Sometimes, by the word 'church' we mean the invisible church, as when we say that 'the *church* is not limited to any one denomination,' meaning true *believers* are found across all denominational lines. Other times we mean the visible church, as when we say, 'We are joining Redeemer *church,*' meaning we are uniting with a particular *congregation.*

Hence, there is confusion. When the Bible speaks of the church, what does it have in mind? The theologians have discerned both of the above uses of the term 'church.' The distinction between the visible and invisible church, on the one hand, is vital, and on the other hand, can be misleading.

INVISIBILITY

Understanding that the true church is invisible and cannot be limited to a particular time or a particular place guards us from a destructive factionalism. I spent some of my childhood and youth in a denomination that believed that it alone was the bride of Christ and it alone would participate in the Marriage Supper of the Lamb (Rev. 19:6-10). Other Christians would be in heaven, we were assured; they just wouldn't be a part of the Supper. Silly as that sounds, it has not been uncommon for ecclesiastical institutions to claim that they alone are the true church and all others are illegitimate or apostate. Rather, the truth is that the true church may be found wherever: 1) the gospel is preached; 2) the sacraments are rightly administered; and 3) ecclesiastical discipline is exercised. These are the three marks that were identified at the time of the Reformation and found in various confessional documents (e.g. *Scots Confession* of 1560). The true church transcends denominational borders.

The doctrine of the church's invisibility also guards us from *spiritual presumption.* What spiritual presumption? The spiritual presumption of those who are still unconverted, but because they are members of the visible church, they think they are saved. Corrie ten Boom of *The Hiding Place* fame cited her father's wisdom in saying, 'Just because a mouse is in the cookie jar doesn't make it a cookie.' Better yet is the Apostle Paul's warning, 'Not all Israel is Israel' (Rom. 9:6). There is an Israel within Israel, a true church within the visible church (see Rom. 9:4-13; 2:25-29). A true believer is a believer 'inwardly,' not merely by outward association, 'a matter of the heart, by the Spirit, not by the letter' (Rom. 2:29). The church in this world contains both wheat and tares, both good fish and bad fish, as Jesus warned, both believer and unbeliever (Matt. 13:36-43; 47-50). Membership in the visible church guarantees nothing. One must also be a member of the church within the church, the church that is invisible in this world.

VISIBILITY

Important as the doctrine of the invisibility of the church is, it can be misleading. How so? Because nearly every reference to the 'church' in the New Testament is to actual congregations. In the book of Acts the word *ecclesia* appears nineteen times, all of which are references to the visible church. The church fears (Acts 5:11), suffers persecution (Acts 8:1, 3; 12:1), prays (Acts 12:5), gathers (Acts 14:27), sends missionaries (Acts 15:3), welcomes guests (Acts 15:4), chooses messengers (Acts 15:22), is strengthened (Acts 15:41; 16:5), greets (Acts 18:22), and appoints elders (Acts 14:23; 20:17) who oversee and care for it (Acts 20:28). It has specific locations such as Jerusalem (Acts 8:1; 11:22), Judea, Galilee, Samaria (Acts 9:31), and Antioch (Acts 11:26; 13:1).

The Apostle Paul addresses his epistles to 'the church in Corinth' (1 Cor. 1:2; 2 Cor. 1:1). He refers to 'the church at Cenchreae' and 'the church that is in their house' (Rom. 16:1, 5; cf. Col. 4:15; Philemon 2); 'the churches of Asia' (1 Cor. 16:19), 'the church of the Laodiceans' (Col. 4:16), and the churches of Galatia

87

(1 Cor. 16:1), Asia (1 Cor. 16:19), and Macedonia (2 Cor. 8:1). He refers to what is taught in 'every church' (1 Cor. 4:17; cf. 11:16; and 14:33) and to 'the churches of God' (1 Cor. 11:16; cf. 11:22), and even what is done 'in church' (1 Cor. 14:35). The ascended Christ (as we have seen) speaks to the 'church in Ephesus,' 'in Smyrna,' 'in Pergamum,' 'in Thyatira,' 'in Sardis,' 'in Philadelphia,' and 'in Laodicea' (Rev. 2:1, 8, 12, 18; 3:1, 7, 14). Churches are said to gather (1 Cor 14:23) and may be 'built up' (1 Cor. 14:4, 5, 12, 19). [1] Get the point? The 'church' is actual congregations made up of actual people in actual places.

It is easy to be committed to an invisible church made up of invisible people. This invisible commitment exposes the flaw in the claim to being committed to the big 'C' Church, the universal and invisible church, while being unattached to any local and visible church. We are meant to express our commitment to the *universal* through the *particular*. A commitment to the 'Church' in a general sense is a commitment to an abstraction, an idea. It requires nothing in particular of me. It allows me in the name of the 'Church' to form my own fellowship group made up of people who look and think remarkably like me, or avoid fellowship with any group at all. In the meantime, I avoid all the headache, all the heartache, all the trials and challenges of an actual congregation made up of a diversity of people, from a diversity of backgrounds and experiences, and having a diversity of

---

1. See also Romans 16:16, 23; 1 Corinthians 7:17, 10:32, 11:18, 22; 12:28; 14:28; 15:9; 16:1; 2 Corinthians 8:18, 19.

ages. This surely is not what Jesus had in mind, or what the Apostles describe. Believers, all believers, are meant to be committed by covenant to a visible church made up of visible people in a visible place.

14

Parachurch or Quasi-church?

A third area of definitional confusion surrounding the word 'church' is common in connection with parachurch organizations. Parachurch groups have played an important role in my spiritual pilgrimage. At one time or another, my spiritual growth has been accelerated by the work of the Row Bible Study at the University of Southern California, Campus Crusade for Christ, InterVarsity Christian Fellowship, Navigators, and Ligonier Ministries. Their Bible studies, small group materials, quiet time aids, and evangelistic tools have been invaluable. Also, a host of non-denominational publishers have placed in my hands the best of Christian literature: Banner of Truth, Zondervan, Baker, Eerdmans, Crossway, and (again) InterVarsity, just to name the most obvious.

Spiritual void filled

In addition, it is obvious to me that a number of parachurch organizations have filled a vacuum left by the negligence of the church. The church wasn't adequately evangelizing the campus, so Campus Crusade stepped in. The church wasn't teaching doctrine, so Ligonier stepped in. The church (especially the mainline church) wasn't teaching the Bible, so Bible Study Fellowship (and its offspring) stepped in. These – and other organizations – have filled the void created by the failure of the church to fulfill its commission. If much of the vital spiritual action in the last seventy-five years has been outside of the church, it largely is because the church has neglected its duty.

Quasi-church

However, this has led to a problem that is obvious to anyone who has been alert. There is a tendency for the *parachurch* to be a *quasi-church*. In other words, the tendency is for the parachurch, for all intents and purposes, to become the functioning church of its participants. It becomes the hub around which the Christian lives of its participants revolve. It is the place to which its people go for fellowship and instruction. Its 'members' are the people to which its participants go in time of crisis. The Bible study, the discipleship group, the prayer group, the Christian organization becomes their church. Participants may still attend a church. Yet practically speaking, the parachurch for them has usurped the church. Their deepest spiritual commitments and their richest Christian fellowship are found outside of the church. The supplanting of the church can and is happening, especially through the internet. An interactive blog can become one's fellowship group. Recordings of sermons can become one's regular diet of preaching. One can, and some are, settling for a 'virtual church.' Post-pandemic, their numbers are growing.

IS THERE A PROBLEM?

Is there a problem with this? Some think not, as long as one is sincerely seeking to follow Christ. As long as one is experiencing fellowship, instruction, and outreach, does it really matter where? they question. How can it be bad? they ask. If people are studying the Bible, if they are praying together, if they are seeking Christian fellowship, why complain? Seems odd that we should raise an objection.

Just as we saw a problem of definitional confusion when speaking of the church when we really mean Christians generally, and when speaking of the visible church when we really mean the invisible church, so also there is a problem of confusing the parachurch organization with the church. The problem, we would say, is that the *para*-church is not the church. That is why these associations and organizations are called 'para' church, meaning 'along-side' the church. They are not meant to rival the church. They are not meant to supplant the church. They are not equipped to replace the church. They *are* meant to aid and assist the church. Their effect should not be to siphon off the church's best people. Their impact should not be to consume the time and energies of the most committed church members to the detriment of the church itself. However, too often this has been the case. The local church often has been weakened by the presence of the parachurch. Who can say

93

if the net result has been positive or negative? We know the positives of parachurch organizations. However, if all those believers whose attention has been occupied by the parachurch group had been pouring their time and energy into the local church, into its burden-bearing fellowship, its body-strengthening teaching, and its soul-saving outreach, what difference might *that* have made?

CHURCH OR PARACHURCH?

Jesus made promises to His church (Matt. 16:18,19; 18:18-20; 28:20; Luke 24:49; Acts 1:8,9). He made no particular promises to parachurch organizations. Just as important, there are qualities of the church that the parachurch group cannot duplicate and, for that reason, it *cannot* replace the church. The parachurch cannot administer the sacraments. Low-church Protestants have at times disparaged the sacraments and denied their importance. However, this makes no sense in light of the Bible. The 'Great Commission' itself includes baptism (Matt. 28:19)! The Apostle Paul associates the Lord's Supper with fellowship, *koinonia* with Christ (1 Cor. 10:16) and describes it as 'spiritual food and... spiritual drink' (1 Cor. 10:3, 4). Can these be neglected without loss?

Moreover, the parachurch organization cannot obligate mutual care and commitment. The church is a covenant community, as we've seen (ch. 10). It always has been a community constituted by covenant, Old Testament and New Testament. One is admitted into it by a covenant sign and vows (circumcision in the Old Testament, baptism in the New) and sustained in it by a covenant meal (Passover in the Old Testament, the Lord's Supper in the New). A *sacramentum,* by definition, was a form of oath-taking required by Roman soldiers. It was the term intentionally chosen by early Christians (the early church father, Tertullian, [c. 155-240] coined the term) to indicate the covenantal nature of these two Christian ordinances. The point is, members are pledged by oath to support and care for each other.

By way of contrast, parachurch participants come and go as they please. The parachurch cannot duplicate the diversity of the church (strong and weak believers, rich and poor believers, cool and uncool believers, etc.), and so cannot duplicate the problematic quality of our mutual commitment. I must commit myself *in the church* to people quite unlike myself, who, at times, I may find undesirable, at least by worldly standards. The parachurch organization is self-selecting. The church is not. I need the diversity of the church in ways I don't need the parachurch group because its diversity forces me to say no to self and to serve without regard to personal advantages to be gained.

Finally, the parachurch cannot require submission to leadership. God has not authorized parachurch leadership to require the submission of other believers to their organization. When they do, things get quite ugly in a hurry. God does not require members of parachurch organizations to be accountable spiritually to leadership and to one another. Yet God does require both submission and accountability in the church quite unambiguously:

> Obey your leaders and submit to them, for they are
> keeping watch over your souls, as those who will have
> to give an account. Let them do this with joy and not
> with groaning, for that would be of no advantage to
> you (Heb. 13:17).

Members of the church 'obey' and 'submit' while leaders
'keep watch.' Leaders are to 'shepherd the flock of God
… exercising oversight … being examples to the flock'
(1 Pet. 5:2-3). Members are to 'respect' leaders who are
'over them' and 'admonish' them (1 Thess. 5:12).

This pattern of submission – accountability cannot
and should not be duplicated in the parachurch
organization. Yet, under the guise of 'mentoring,' we
see more and more even of this happening. Outside of
ecclesiastical authority, outside of the direction of church
officers, self-appointed mentors are exercising heavy-
handed guidance over other believers. To whom are these
mentors accountable? All too often, no one.

Bottom-line

Don't let the *parachurch* become a *quasi-church*. Don't let
it become the unit of fellowship. Don't let it become the
source of instruction. Don't let it become the agent of
accountability. Don't let it divert time and energy away
from the church. We need the church. The parachurch
organization, however, is not the church. The parachurch
has filled a void and done considerable good. However,
without *the* church, the *parachurch* has nothing to stand
alongside of. Truth be known, as an organization, it
needs the church as much as each of us do individually.

15
Hypocrites at Church

In addition to definitional confusion, there are other reasons why the church is regarded in a diminished light. We need to respond to these. The most common reason for refusing to be involved in church, or even attend, is the bad behavior of its members. Hypocrisy, in a word, is the obstacle. One has been hurt by the negligence or harshness or cruelty of a member. Perhaps another has been turned off by the political views or social or moral views that one perceives characterize a given congregation. Still a third has become disillusioned by the dishonesty or vulgarity or immorality of members: perhaps a member who is a church leader, a member who dresses up nicely on Sunday, who looks the part, talks the part, plays the part on the church grounds, but behaves poorly all week long. Sadly, this member, who pretends to be one thing on Sunday, is quite a different person throughout the week.

The discrepancy between the ideal church and the actual church, Christians as they are supposed to be and

Christians as they are, is so troubling for some people that they simply quit. They stop coming. They want nothing to do with church. They don't want to be anywhere near that hypocrite or those many hypocrites and their bad behavior and bad thoughts.

EVER THUS

What can we say about this? Simply this: the church is made up of people. People, Christian people, redeemed people, church people, are still people. People do bad things. They always have and they always will. That is why the bad behavior of members should never become the criteria for determining our personal level of involvement in the life of the church. If it were, we would *never* darken the church's doors, simply because there are a host of bad people there. This is always the case and always has been.

The Apostle Peter had to deal with the deception of Ananias and Sapphira (Acts 5:1-11) and the covetousness of Simon the Magician (Acts 8:9-24). The Apostle Paul constantly had to defend himself from the attacks of other believers who, out of 'envy and rivalry' and 'selfish ambition,' falsely accused him of one thing or another (Phil. 1:15-18; Gal. 1:10; 4:16-17; 6:13; 2 Cor. 10:9-12). He was abandoned by Phygelus and Hermogenes (2 Tim. 1:15), deserted by Demas (2 Tim. 4:10), and greatly harmed by Alexander the coppersmith (2 Tim. 4:14). The Apostle John had to deal with Diotrephes, 'who loves to have the preeminence' (3 John 9 NKJV). Advance warning was given by the

Apostle Paul to the Ephesian elders of the 'fierce wolves' who would 'come in among you, not sparing the flock.' Bad men would arise 'from among your own selves,' from among the elders, who would speak 'twisted things' in order to 'draw away the disciples after them' (Acts 20:29,30). Jude warns of 'certain people' who 'crept in unnoticed,' who pervert grace and deny Christ (Jude 4). It has been ever thus! We repeat: the church has always been a mixed multitude of wheat and tares which grow up together and cannot be separated until the last day (Matt. 13:36-43). Drag a gospel net through an ocean of humanity, Jesus warns, and both good and bad 'fish' will be caught (Matt. 13:47-50).

EXPECTATIONS

In many areas of life, the *ideal* can become the enemy of the *achievable*. For example, expectations in marriage are crucial. If I am expecting unending marital bliss from the moment I marry and instead, encounter periodic doses of tension, disagreement, and discouragement, I may conclude that I married the wrong person and leave. If I am realistic about what is achievable in marriage between two children of Adam, I will take marital conflict in my stride. The key is, what am I expecting? If I have utopian expectations for my country, I will find occasions for disillusionment at every turn. Ideals are good to have. Yet they should always be held in the context of the achievable. This is the wisdom behind the quip of Churchill (and I paraphrase), 'Democracy is the worst form of government, except for all the rest.' The same could be said of the United States. It is the worst, the most evil nation on earth, except for all the rest. Compared to the ideal, it fails. However, compared to the history and achievements of every other nation across the globe, compared to what nations and peoples actually do, compared to what is achievable in the collective entities we call nations, there are compelling reasons to be thankful for what we have.

The failings of the German church during the Hitler era were considerable. The so-called 'German Christianity' was horribly compromised and a disgrace to the name Christian. Yet the German church, particularly the 'Confessing Church' of the faithful, failed compared to what? Albert Einstein, no less, wrote *commending* the German church for its resistance to Hitler. He compared the church not to a standard of perfection, but to the other institutions of German society: the press, the universities, the politicians, the army, big business, the labor unions, which all capitulated, while faithful Lutherans and Catholics continued to resist right to the end.

Jesus' church

The disciples of Christ are not perfected in this world. Sanctification is a lifelong project. Likewise, the disciples of Christ as a collective entity, as a church, are not perfected. The church is not perfected. It will remain deeply flawed until Jesus returns. This is by God's design; however, His purposes may seem odd to us. He does not intend to perfect us until glory. In the meantime, we all stumble, fall, and fail.

This is why the bad behavior or bad opinions of members should never be allowed to become the criteria by which I determine my involvement or non-involvement. If it were a valid criterion, the church could never have been formed. As C. H. Spurgeon once said (again, I paraphrase), 'If you find the perfect church, don't join it, you'll ruin it.' Exactly. The very concept of the church means that bad people like me have to join with and put up with bad people like you. We all bring our baggage with us into the church where it causes problems. No wonder we have to be told, 'Be kind to one another, tenderhearted, forgiving one another, as God in Christ forgave you' (Eph. 4:32). The hypocrisy of Christians is more of an excuse than an explanation for abandoning the church.

16
Denominationalism

When our two older sons, Drew and Sam, were little boys, we periodically traveled to Greenville to visit grandparents 'Netsi' and 'Bop-Bop.' On one occasion they arranged a trip for the boys to the fire station. The firemen were kind to the little fellows, showing them their equipment and asking them questions about themselves. Upon learning that our family was from Savannah, Georgia, one of the firemen concluded of our major league baseball allegiances, 'You must be Atlanta Braves' fans.' Drew immediately responded, 'No, sir. We're Presbyterians.'

Amusing as that story is, no doubt some believers might be horrified. They might conclude that our children were victims of an over-hyped denominationalism, yet another reason given for a diminished regard for the church. Throughout the twentieth century and to the present day, a growing number of Christians began to see denominations as a liability rather than as an asset. Denominations are seen by them as representing petty divisions within Christianity and little else. Hence, the impetus to belong to a church that claims no denominational affiliation and is merely 'Christian.' Nondenominational Protestants are now the second largest group of American Protestants, after Baptists and ahead of Methodists and Pentecostals. So desirable has a nondenominational identity become that many denominational churches mask their denominational identity, calling themselves 'Saddleback Church' (though a Southern Baptist congregation) or 'Grace Church' (though a Presbyterian Church in America). Most so-called 'community' churches (are other churches not a part of the community in which they are located?) are either nondenominational or intentionally hiding their denominational brand. When denominational labels are dropped, a church is able to project the message that says, 'We care about what unifies Christians, not what divides them. We emphasize the important things that believers hold in common, not the secondary or even trivial matters that separate.'

Old school

This has not been our approach in Savannah; rather, the opposite is the case. We tend to fly our denominational flags. We *highlight* rather than *hide* our denominational identity. We think being Presbyterian is important. We think the distinctive set of beliefs and practices that make a Presbyterian a Presbyterian are worth preserving – and even promoting. We think that when one leaves Presbyterianism for another brand of Christianity, one loses something important. We would expect to hear the same from Anglicans, Baptists, and others. This is not to say that we don't have much in common with other Christian bodies. When we recite the Creed each week, we demonstrate the value we place on truly catholic (small 'c') Christianity. Yet what a nondenominational branding implies, we cannot affirm. What might that be? That one considers the sacraments, church government, form of worship, eschatology, and predestination/sovereignty of God, the issues over which most denominational divisions occur, as secondary issues?

If we focus on just the first of these, the sacraments, it is unprecedented in the 2,000-year history of the Christian church to regard the sacraments as of secondary importance. Christians of previous eras were willing to die for their particular understanding of the Lord's Supper. Blood was shed over whether the transubstantiation, consubstantiation, true (spiritual) presence, or no particular presence best describes the nature of Christ's presence in the Lord's Supper. Or take another issue, church government. When oppressive church bureaucracies are suffocating some churches and unaccountable preacher-dictators controlling others, is this really the time to be saying that the form of church government doesn't matter? Or, consider worship. Given the anarchy, given the pervasive chaos, given the continuing conflict over worship, is this really wise to say it doesn't matter how one worships? Is someone really going to claim this, even in light of the teaching of the Bible and 2,000 years of church history?

Separating the primary from the secondary is a notoriously difficult task. The interrelatedness of the whole body of Christian truth makes identifying so-called core or main or central doctrines problematic. One may think that the doctrine of God's sovereignty is esoteric, but try withholding Romans 8:28 from someone whose family has just suffered a terrible tragedy. Is God working *this* for their good or not? Does He have a purpose in this or is it without purpose? without meaning? merely a matter of bad luck? The point is, we are not just Christian. We are Presbyterian. When we start new churches, we start Presbyterian churches. When we support overseas missions, we support Presbyterian missions. When we move to a new community, we look for a Presbyterian church. When we send our children to college, we look for a Reformed institution or a Reformed campus organization. Again, we would expect Baptists, Methodists, Lutherans, and Anglicans to do the same. Why? Because our distinctive beliefs and practices matter.

I understand why people say, 'The main things are the plain things.' There is no need to fight over everything. There is no need to give equal time to the most remote doctrines. C. S. Lewis likens 'mere Christianity' to a large hall in which all Christians may gather. Leading out from the main hall are multiple doors opening into several rooms. These are the various denominations. One room is Episcopal. Another is Lutheran. Another is Baptist, and so on. It is in these side-rooms, he concedes, that all the important action takes place. 'It is in the rooms, not in the hall, that there are fires and chairs and meals.'[1] The main hall, common Christianity, is that to which evangelism aims: we wish to bring the unbelieving to Christ, to the Christian faith. However, one must not remain in the main hall. Convictions must be recognized and honored regarding God, humanity, sin, salvation, the church, the Christian life, and the last days, and not treated with indifference. The process of settling one's convictions moves one through an adjoining door and into a distinctive denominational room. It is there that Bible study occurs. It is there that fellowship is experienced. It is there that mutual care takes place. It is there that spiritual fires warm the soul.

It is ironic that nondenominational churches, for all their nondenominationalism, can be pegged denominationally in a matter of five minutes with a dozen or less questions. Indeed, most of the nondenominational churches are credo-baptist and dispensational in belief and practice. Most would fit comfortably in the Southern Baptist Convention. They only pretend to be nondenominational. And that is okay, so long as reality is recognized. The reality is, they are as theologically denominational as anyone.

---

1. C. S. Lewis, *Mere Christianity* (1952; New York: Harper Collins, 2001), xv.

IV
Historic Perspectives

17
Mother Church

Years ago, I watched a series of interviews on the television of inmates at the state prison. They were asked about their background, their family life, their parents. Several of them mentioned what losers their fathers were: harsh, cruel, negligent, philandering, drunks, etc. Yet, without exception, they warmly commended their mothers. 'She was a good woman,' they'd say. Or, 'She had a good heart.' According to a recent biographer, William Fox (1879-1952), founder of Fox Film (which would eventually merge into movie giant Twentieth Century Fox) hated his father, who was an adulterer and indifferent to his children. When his father died, he cursed his corpse and spat on his coffin. Yet he adored his mother.[1] Why the contrast? Because with few exceptions, mother-love prevails. Those who bear, birth and nurture children establish a bond with those children that perseveres. Even hardened criminals,

---

1. See Scott Eyman, 'A Pioneer and Overreacher,' review article of Vanda Krefft, *The Man Who Made the Movies* (2017), *Wall Street Journal,* Dec. 9-10, 2017, C-6.

calloused to all that is good and worthwhile, recognize the depth and beauty of maternal love and appreciate it. The unparalleled strength of it lies behind the rhetorical question of Isaiah 49:15:

> Can a woman forget her nursing child,
>   that she should have no compassion on the
>   son of her womb?
> Even these may forget,
>   yet I will not forget you.

The Reformers enthusiastically employed the metaphor of motherhood found in Galatians 4:26 ('the Jerusalem above ... is our mother'). The church, says Luther in his *Large Catechism,* 'is the mother that brings to birth and sustains every Christian through the Word of God.'[2] Calvin entitles Book IV of the *Institutes,* 'The true Church, and the Necessity of our Union with Her, *Being the Mother of all the Faithful.*'[3] Calvin said of the *visible* (not the invisible) church,

> [L]et us learn even from the simple title 'mother' how useful, indeed how necessary, it is that we should know [the church]. For there is no other way to enter life unless this mother conceive us in her womb, give us birth, nourish us at her breast, and lastly, unless she keep us under her care and guidance until, putting off mortal flesh, we become like the angels. Our weakness

---

2. Martin Luther, *Luther's Large Catechism* (Minneapolis, MN; Augsburg Publishing House, 1935, 122).

3. This is the wording of the Allen edition of the *Institutes* (1844; Philadelphia: Presbyterian Board of Christian Education, 1949), 269 (my emphasis), which is obscured in the McNeill edition.

does not allow us to be dismissed from her school until we have been pupils all our lives. Furthermore, away from her bosom one cannot hope for any forgiveness of sins or any salvation.[4]

'Note that the church, here called 'Mother,' is the *visible* church,' says John McNeill in his footnotes accompanying the standard translation of the *Institutes*, 'and that the mother function of the church, bearing and nourishing believers, *is necessary to salvation*.'[5] 'The church,' says Calvin in his commentary on Ephesians 4:11-13, 'is the common mother of all the godly, which bears, nourishes, and governs in the Lord both kings and commoners; and this is done by the ministry.'[6] Calvin endorsed another of Cyprian's sayings, 'that he who would have God as his father *must have the church as his mother*.'

Puritan authors regularly utilized the nourishing metaphor of motherhood, portraying the believer as a child nursing at the breasts of mother church, those breasts representing the means of grace. 'Lie sucking at

4. John Calvin, *Institutes of the Christian Religion* – Vol. I & II, in John T. McNeill (ed.) The Library of Christian Classics, Volume XXI. (Philadelphia: The Westminster Press, 1960), IV.1.4.

5. Ibid., 1016, note 10 (my emphasis).

6. John Calvin, *The Epistles of Paul the Apostle to the Galatians, Ephesians, Philippians and Colossians,* Calvin's New Testament Commentaries, ed. David W. and Thomas F. Torrance (Grand Rapids: William B. Eerdmans Publishing Co., 1965), 181; For Calvin, Ephesians 4:11-12 'was perhaps *the* critical text for the biblical doctrine of ministry,' says Calvin scholar Elsie Anne McKee (cited in John W. Tweeddale, 'The Church as Mother,' in Derek W. H. Thomas and John W. Tweeddale, (eds.), *John Calvin: For a New Reformation* (Wheaton: Crossway, 2019, 475). Similar statements by Calvin can be found in his commentaries at Galatians 4:26 and 1 Timothy 3:15.

this breast,' says William Gurnall (1617-1679) of the ordinances of the church in his classic, *The Christian in Complete Armour*, 'and that often.'[7] John Cotton (1584-1652), minister of First Church, Boston, published in 1646 a catechism for children entitled *Milk for Babes: Drawn Out of the Breasts of Both Testaments*, a work which remained in print for over 200 years.[8] This is typical of Reformed Protestantism.

The Apostle Paul himself utilizes the maternal metaphor in describing his own ministry.

> But we were gentle among you, like a nursing mother taking care of her own children (1 Thess. 2:7, cf. Gal. 4:26).

Believers are likened to 'newborn infants' who 'long for the pure spiritual milk' which, of course, newborns access from their mothers (1 Pet. 2:2). The metaphor of mother church, from which believers draw their vital sustenance, is fully justified from Scripture. Mother church conceives and carries us, and bears us in her womb and feeds us at her breasts. Her love for us, our dependence upon her, and our indebtedness to her demands our loving affection in return. What we owe to our natural mothers we owe to our spiritual mother as well. This means not merely an annual 'Mother's Day' card. It means a consistent pattern of gratitude, care, provision, and service. A higher doctrine of the visible

---

7. William Gurnall, *The Christian in Complete Armour*, (1662 and 1665; Edinburgh: The Banner of Truth Trust, 1964), II:56.

8. *Electronic Texts in American Studies*. Paper 18.

church, lest it be the overwrought Roman Catholic one, is hardly imaginable. D. G. Hart, in his book *Recovering Mother Kirk*, rightly urges Presbyterians 'to abandon the notion of the church as personal trainer' and to recover 'Calvin's idea of the church as mother.'[9]

9. D. G. Hart, *Recovering Mother Kirk: The Case for Liturgy in the Reformed Tradition* (Grand Rapids: Baker Academic, 2003), 39.

18

Slighting the Church

What does the Bible have to say to those who purposefully remove themselves from the fellowship of the visible church, perhaps claiming of orthodox churches their insufficient purity or some other inadequacy? What Reformed Protestants have taught about neglecting what they would call 'public ordinances' is sobering. Those today who absent themselves from the assembly, who content themselves with the electronic 'church,' or with a coffee-shop Bible study, or home-church, or no church, take heed.

Let's allow Calvin to be our guide. He warns that 'God's fatherly favor and especial witness of spiritual life are limited to his flock.' He warns those looking for God's blessing outside of the church: don't do it. 'It is always disastrous to leave the (visible) church,' he insists.[1] He expounds Ephesians 4:11ff, noting that God has entrusted both the means of grace and gifted individuals to equip and mature the saints and build up the body

---

1. Calvin, *Institutes,* IV.i.4.

of Christ. Calvin acknowledges that God could 'perfect his own' immediately without means. 'Nevertheless (He) desires them to grow up into manhood solely under the direction of the church.'[2] Consequently, 'It follows that all those who spurn the spiritual food, divinely extended to them through the hand of the church, deserve to perish in famine and hunger.' 'Recognize,' he urges us, 'it is his will to teach us through human means.'[3] Calvin laments the 'unholy separation' of those who 'are led either by pride, dislike, or rivalry to the conviction that they can profit enough from private reading and meditation; hence they despise public assemblies and deem preaching superfluous.'[4]

Slighting the church, we see, is not a new problem! 'Woe to their pride,' Calvin warns those 'who think that for them the private reading is enough, and that they have no need of the common ministry of the Church.'[5] Realize, he urges, 'Believers have no greater help than public worship.'[6] Whenever the true gospel is preached and the sacraments are rightly administered, there the true church exists, 'even if it otherwise swarms with many faults.'[7] Where it exists, 'No one is permitted to spurn its authority, flout its warnings, resist its counsels,

---

2. Ibid., IV.i.5.

3. Ibid.

4. Ibid.

5. Calvin, *Commentary on Ephesians,* 181.

6. Calvin, *Institutes,* IV.i.5.

7. Ibid., IV.i.11.

or make light of its chastisements – much less to desert it and break its unity.'

> For the Lord esteems the communion of His church so highly that He counts as traitor and apostate from Christianity anyone who arrogantly leaves any Christian society, provided it cherishes the true ministry of Word and sacraments.[8]

Stronger still: 'Separation from the church *is the denial of Christ and God.*'[9] More simply from the Apostle John: 'They went out from us ... that it might become plain that *they all are not of us*' (1 John 2:19).

The visible church is given pastors and teachers called and gifted by God for ministry (Eph. 4:11ff). These gifted men are tasked with administering the means of grace (word, sacraments and prayer), likewise given to the visible church, whereby sinners are saved and saints are sanctified. Outside this realm of ministers and ministry, this realm of salvation, is another realm, the realm of Satan and destruction (1 Cor. 5:5; cf. Matt. 18:17). Given our 'collapsing ecclesiology' today, is it not vital that this message of the indispensability of the church be broadcast far and wide?

---

8. Ibid., IV.i.10.

9. Ibid., (my emphasis). Similarly, see above Second Helvetic Confession (1562) and the Belgic Confession (1561) which warns, 'no person ... ought to draw himself, to live in a separate state from it; but that all men are in duty bound to join and unite themselves with it' (*The Creeds of Christendom: With a History and Critical Notes,* Ed. Philip Schaff, Rev. David S. Schaff, Vol III, "The Evangelical Protestant Creeds" [1931; Grand Rapids: Baker Book House, 1985]).

19
Sola Ecclesia: A Sixth Sola?

We have seen that Jesus sums up His entire ministry, the central aim behind His incarnation, life, death, resurrection, ascension, session, intercession, and return, as building His church (Matt. 16:18-20). The church He is building is a visible institution that has accountability, members, standards of belief and conduct, means of inclusion and exclusion, a method of discipline, and a form of government. It has the power of 'binding and loosing' and the 'keys of the kingdom' (Matt. 16:18-20; Matt. 18:18-20). It is His *body* (1 Cor. 12:4ff; Rom. 12:4, 5) and His *wife-bride* (Eph. 5:22ff; Rev. 21:9; 19:9; Song of Solomon; Ps. 45). It is our mother (Gal. 4:26; 1 Pet. 2:2). Its members are to love one another and bear each other's burdens (John 13:34, 35; Gal. 6:1,2). The excuses for the neglect of the church, its ineffectiveness, its hypocrisy, and its petty denominational divisions are excuses, not adequate explanations.

This leads us to a question that we wish to ask. Should there be a sixth 'sola'?[1] The five 'solas' are universally

---

1. We are not the first to ask this question. See John R. Muether, 'A Sixth Sola?' in *Modern Reformation*, August 2, 2007; Bruce Atkinson, 'The

recognized Reformation mottos that continue to clarify crucial Protestant distinctives today: *sola scriptura* (scripture alone is our final rule of faith and practice); *solo Christo* (Christ's atonement and mediation provide the sole *ground* of our salvation); *sola fide* (faith alone is the *instrument* by which salvation is received); *sola gratia* (God's grace is the ultimate *cause* of our salvation); *soli Deo Gloria* (God's glory is the final *aim* in all His and our endeavors).[2] The proposed sixth *sola* is this: *sola ecclesia,* the church alone, meaning salvation may be found in the church alone.[3]

No doubt this proposal would, and should, raise eyebrows. Roman Catholics used the motto *sola ecclesia* to refer to the church's final authority to determine orthodox doctrine. The church, it has been argued – and continues to be argued – sits over both Holy Writ and the Holy Tradition of which it is the sole caretaker. It alone, through its teaching magisterium, can formulate from these two sources the theology and practice of the faithful. One seeking

---

Seven Solas,' in *Virtueonline,* Dec. 31, 2009; Michael J. Glodo, 'Sola Ecclesia: The Lost Reformation Doctrine,' *Reformation and Revival,* Vol. 19, No. 4, Fall 2000. The question has also been entertained by Kevin J. Vanhoozer, *Biblical Authority After Babel: Retrieving the Solas in the Spirit of Mere Protestant Christianity* (Grand Rapids: Brazos Press, 2016), 29, 176, 198, 211.

2. While these five 'solas' date to the Reformation, there is no evidence for their being brought together in a single place until the 20th century (see Vanhoozer, *Biblical Authority After Babel,* 26).

3. By *sola ecclesia,* Vanhoozer means 'the church alone is the place where Christ rules over his kingdom and gives certain gifts for the building of his living temple' (*Biblical Authority After Babel,* 29).

to understand how the Roman Catholics have come to believe in Mary's Immaculate Conception, her bodily assumption, or her titles of co-Mediator and co-Redeemer with Christ need look no further. True, they are not found in the Bible, yet they need not be. They are part of the authoritative tradition of the church.

Nevertheless, the proposal of 'Sola Ecclesia' should be considered by Reformed Protestants in the first instance because it provides the context within which the other solas ordinarily are operative. This was especially evident as we looked carefully at 'Jesus and the Church.' We are saved by sovereign *grace alone*, yet Christ has given the means *of grace* to the church: that is, the word, sacraments, and prayer. We are saved by *faith alone*; a faith, however, which doesn't leave us alone but unites us to Christ *and* to each other, the church being a creature of the word. *Christ alone* is the Savior and Lord of the church, yet He gives to the church the keys that open the doors of His kingdom (Matt. 16:18). *Scripture alone* is the final authority for faith and practice, yet Christ appoints officers in the church to exercise His authority, giving them the power of binding and loosing, even of forgiving or retaining sin (Matt. 16:18-20; Matt. 18:18-20; John 20:23). Salvation takes place in and through the ministry of the church alone.

NO SALVATION OUTSIDE

Once one sees that the ministry of the gospel (as represented by the mottos) is operative primarily in the church, it is easy to see why the Reformers would have endorsed the church father Cyprian's (A.D. 200-258) doctrine that 'there is no salvation outside of the church.' There is no hesitation in this regard among the Reformers or in the Reformed Church. John R. Muether has collected a number of classic Protestant confessional statements to prove the point.[4] Luther, in his Large Catechism (1529), writes, 'But outside the Christian church (that is, where the Gospel is not) there is no forgiveness, and hence no holiness … Therefore they remain in eternal wrath and damnation … Outside of [the Christian church] no one can come to the Lord Jesus.'[5] Calvin's Geneva Catechism (1542) teaches the same:

> Minister: Why do you subjoin the forgiveness of sins to the Church?
>
> Child: Because no one obtains it, unless he has previously been united with the people of God, cultivates this unity with the body of Christ up to the end, and thus testifies that he is a true member of the Church.
>
> Minister: You conclude from this that outside the Church there is no salvation but only damnation and ruin?

---

4. See also Ryan M. McGraw, *The Ark of Safety: Is There Salvation Outside of the Church?* (Grand Rapids: Reformation Heritage Books, 2018).

5. See Muether, 'A Sixth Sola?', cf. *Dr. Martin Luther's Large Catechism* (Minneapolis: Augsburg Publishing House, 1935), 126.

Child: Certainly. Those who disrupt from the body of Christ and split its unity into schisms, are quite excluded from the hope of salvation, so long as they remain in dissidence of this kind.[6]

'No one can be saved out of the Church,' Zacharias Ursinus (1534-1583) insists in his *Commentary on the Heidelberg Catechism*. Why? 'Because outside the church there is no Saviour, and hence no salvation.'[7] Similarly, in the Second Helvetic Confession of 1562 (Swiss Reformed Church), written by Zwingli's successor at Zurich, Henry Bullinger (1504-1575), we read: 'we deny that those can live before God who do not stand in fellowship with the true Church of God, but separate themselves from it.'[8] The Belgic Confession of 1561 (Dutch Reformed Church) teaches that the church is 'an assembly of those who are saved, and outside of it there is no salvation.' Consequently, 'No person of whatsoever state or condition he may be, ought to withdraw himself, to live in a separate state from it' (Article 28).[9] Finally, Presbyterianism's *Westminster Confession of Faith* (1648) maintains that outside of the visible church 'there is no

---

6. Muether, 'A Sixth Sola?', cf. John Calvin, *Selected Works of John Calvin, Vol. 2: Tracts and Letters,* Henry Beveridge and Jules Bonnet (eds.) (1849; Grand Rapids, Baker Book House, 1983), 52.

7. Zacharias Ursinus, *Commentary on the Heidelberg Catechism* (1562, 1852; Phillipsburg, New Jersey: Presbyterian and Reformed Publishing Co., n/d), 292.

8. *The Book of Confessions* (Atlanta: The Office of the General Assembly of the Presbyterian Church [USA], 1985), 5.136.

9. Philip Schaff (ed.), *The Creeds of Christendom,* Volumes I-III (1931; Grand Rapids: Baker Book House Company, 1985), III:418.

ordinary possibility of salvation' (XXV.2). The various nineteenth century commentaries on the *Westminster Confession of Faith* (e.g. Shaw, A. A. Hodge) and twentieth and twenty-first century (Williamson, Van Dixhoorn, Fesko) affirm the same. This is the characteristic conviction of post-Reformation Reformed theologians.

Let's return now to the setting in which we began our discussion of the doctrine of the church. It's Sunday morning. My wake-up routine has been completed. What am I now to do? Here is my answer. Do what the Scriptures require and what Christians have done for 2,000 years. Go to the public assembly, gathered under the discipline of Christ's appointed officers to be ministered to by the word read, preached, sung, prayed, and displayed in the sacraments. Gather with those who, with you, compose the body and the bride of Christ in a given location and to whom you are joined by covenant. Doing so is crucial to your personal spiritual health and the well-being of the Christian community. Once there, fulfill your responsibility to love and care for the brethren. God's people should consider no other alternative, should desire no other option.

The Primary Mission of the Church
Engaging or Transforming the World?
Bryan D. Estelle

This book has four parts. Part one gives the biblical basis for the primary mission of the Church. Part two of this book explores what the primary mission of the Church is not. Part three of this book pivots toward a positive definition of what the primary mission of the Church is. Part four is more practical. In the final three chapters (part four) of the book, the discussion turns to several areas where the Scripture's teach about ecclesiology, specifically on the primary mission of the Church. The book now assumes a practical import for her practice: the nature and limitations of Church power, the mission of the Church and politics and education.

Finally, the book concludes with the famous biblical passage in which Paul addresses Athenian citizens on the Aeropagus. This sublime sermon exemplifies Paul's exquisite evangelism and ably pictures and embodies the positive principles in this book on the primary mission of the Church. Throughout, Estelle argues that the mission of the corporate Church is spiritual, which means that he describes those things that are properly of and properly belonging to the Church.

ISBN: 978-1-5271-0776-2

Christian Focus Publications

Our mission statement –

STAYING FAITHFUL

In dependence upon God we seek to impact the world through literature faithful to His infallible Word, the Bible. Our aim is to ensure that the Lord Jesus Christ is presented as the only hope to obtain forgiveness of sin, live a useful life and look forward to heaven with Him.

Our Books are published in four imprints:

CHRISTIAN
FOCUS

popular works including biographies, commentaries, basic doctrine and Christian living.

CHRISTIAN
HERITAGE

books representing some of the best material from the rich heritage of the church.

MENTOR

books written at a level suitable for Bible College and seminary students, pastors, and other serious readers. The imprint includes commentaries, doctrinal studies, examination of current issues and church history.

CF4•K

children's books for quality Bible teaching and for all age groups: Sunday school curriculum, puzzle and activity books; personal and family devotional titles, biographies and inspirational stories – because you are never too young to know Jesus!

Christian Focus Publications Ltd,
Geanies House, Fearn, Ross-shire,
IV20 1TW, Scotland, United Kingdom.
www.christianfocus.com